From the Stone Age to Thomas Merton

From the Stone Age to Thomas Merton

A Short History of Contemplative Prayer

LARRY HART

Foreword by James Farris

WIPF & STOCK • Eugene, Oregon

FROM THE STONE AGE TO THOMAS MERTON
A Short History of Contemplative Prayer

Copyright © 2018 Larry Hart. All rights reserved. Except for brief quotations in critical publications or reviews, no part of this book may be reproduced in any manner without prior written permission from the publisher. Write: Permissions, Wipf and Stock Publishers, 199 W. 8th Ave., Suite 3, Eugene, OR 97401.

Wipf & Stock
An Imprint of Wipf and Stock Publishers
199 W. 8th Ave., Suite 3
Eugene, OR 97401

www.wipfandstock.com

PAPERBACK ISBN: 978-1-5326-5268-4
HARDCOVER ISBN: 978-1-5326-5269-1
EBOOK ISBN: 978-1-5326-5270-7

Manufactured in the U.S.A.   09/07/18

Excerpt from "East Coker" from COLLECTED POEMS (1909–1962) by T.S. Eliot. Copyright 1936 by Hooughton Mifflin Harcourt Publishing Company. All rights reserved.

New American Standard Bible, copyright 1960, 1962, 1963, 1968, 1971, 1972, 1973, 1975, 1977, 1995 by The Lockman Foundation.

New Revised Standard Version with the Apocrypha copyright 1991, 1994 by Oxford University Press.

The Holy Bible: Contemporary English Version, copyright 1995 by American Bible Society.

The Holy Bible: New International Version, copyright 1978 by New York International Bible Society.

The Message, copyright 1993, 1994, 1995, 1996, 2000, 2002 by NavPress Publishing Group.

The New English Version, copyright 1961 by Oxford University Press and Cambridge University Press.

Revised English Bible with the Apocrypha, copyright 1989 by Oxford University Press and Cambridge University Press.

I dedicate this book, which I intend as my last, to my family of origin—immediate and extended:

My mother and father: Jewell and Herman J. Hart.

My siblings: Barbara (Bobbie), Yvonne (Nonnie), and Tom (Sonny).

My nieces and nephews: Patricia (Trish) and Bob (Bobby), Jerry Dale and Tawnya, and Maurine and Kathryn.

The two grown children Brenda and I have: Larry (Donnie) and Carolyn.

My grandparents: Tom and Lydia Downs and William and Maud Hart, and all the aunts and uncles with which the latter two provided my childhood.

If you wish. If you wish, you can be trained. You can become knowledgeable if you give your mind to it. If you enjoy listening you will learn. And you can become wise if you are attentive. Trained, knowledgeable, and wise if you wish it, if you give your mind to it, if you are attentive.

Ecclesiasticus 6:32–33

Contents

Acknowledgments | ix
Abbreviations | x
Foreword by James Farris | xi
Introduction | xvii

ONE
The Invention of Contemplative Prayer: The Stone Age | 1

TWO
Contemplative Prayer and the Old Testament | 14

THREE
Contemplative Prayer and the New Testament | 26

FOUR
Contemplative Prayer and Monasticism | 43

FIVE
Contemplative Prayer and Contemporary Christianity | 60

SIX
Some Final Observations | 72

SEVEN
It's Easier Than You Think | 89

Epilogue

Bibliography | 101

Acknowledgments

THANK YOU TO THE usual suspects: Brenda, my wife, our daughter Carolyn, and our dear friends Ruth Ann Lee and Allison DeLong. They are always so generous with their help. And I don't know what I would do without Carolyn's technical support. Thanks to the Rev. Esther Diane Smith, PhD, for reading and commenting on the manuscript. I am also grateful for Jack, who keeps me quiet company as I write—napping on the floor beside me or placing a paw on my leg to let me know it's time for the noon prayers, to take a walk, and maybe have a little lunch.

Abbreviations

CEV	Contemporary English Version
MSG	The Message
NASB	New American Standard Bible
NEV	New English Version
NIV	New International Version
NRSV	New Revised Standard Version
REB	Revised English Version

Foreword

FATHER JAMES FARRIS

WHAT DOES IT MEAN to be a Christian? The question should haunt everyone who is serious about his or her faith. It is not answered in a single response. Instead, it is a question which repeats itself each day. We are like the first disciples wondering at the works of Jesus. The words and works of the Master brought the question: "Who can this be" (Luke 8:25)?

We can learn new ways of looking at faith if we utilize wisdom wherever we find it. One bit of wisdom is given by the great Zen teacher, Shunryu Suzuki, who has a lesson we can use for this question of the identity of Jesus. Suzuki taught his students this principle: "In the beginner's mind there are many possibilities. In the expert's mind there are few."[1] He urged his students to maintain the mind of the beginner. So too, with our Christian faith in Jesus Christ, we must continuously have the mind of a beginner if we are to know the truth and be set free (John 8:32). How does faith set us free? How does Christ set us free?

And what shall we be freed of? This is another question for beginners in the faith—for all of us. For we should all have the mind of the novice. We can answer that we are freed of our sins, freed of death, freed of blind self-will, or of our compulsive behaviors. This is the hope and substance of our faith. Yet the heart of the Christian experience lies somewhere beyond catechism answers to the meaning of faith, lies beyond the limits of all words.

1. Suzuki, *Zen Mind, Beginner's Mind*, 21.

Foreword

The path of faith and freedom is given in Hebrews 12:2 with these words: "Keep your eyes fixed on Jesus, the author and perfecter of our faith." We fix our eyes on Jesus to move beyond ideas through the encounter called prayer. This is a promise of freedom because we are taken beyond the limits of our own opinions and definitions, like the bloom of first love in adolescence. When we first fall in love, we are in a new place, experiencing a freedom that can be both confusing and blissful. It is like the descriptions of so many masters of prayer in the history of spirituality.

Prayer is knowledge beyond thought, for it is different from thinking about a subject. Instead of thoughts about God, it is a reach for God—a desire to be one with God. It may begin with words, but it quickly moves the focus to the desire of the heart—beyond words. Throughout the history of Judaism and Christianity, prayer is often described in erotic terms: the lover and the Beloved, being ravished by God, passion and fulfillment. But like human love stories, it also involves anguish, emptiness and doubt. This is the thread of contemplative Christian prayer, from even before the beginning of Christianity—the long history of spiritual writers, saints and teachers. Such prayer is the future path of Christian faith if Christianity is to thrive, especially in the postmodern Western world.

Christendom is being rapidly dismantled in the West. Throughout Europe, and in much of America, new generations bring skepticism to any practice of faith. The structures of the Christian church are challenged by a secular society, and its challenges are not all unfounded. Christian churches are seeing a constant drop in Sunday attendance and in membership. Young people ask why faith is necessary at all, and old answers are shown to be unsatisfying. Christian faith was seen as the path for moral behavior by previous generations, yet war, violence, political infighting, and the moral failures of the church have become a scandal to the young, prompting them to believe that morality can be achieved without religious practice. There is something to be said for this assertion because even St. Paul reminds us in the Letter to the Romans that morality is natural to the human heart. Christian

Foreword

faith blossoms in moral and compassionate behavior, but its seeds are the experience of a new presence and a new consciousness. The communal and personal life of prayer unveils this presence as "the mystery that was hidden for ages and generations but now revealed to His saints... which is Christ in you, the hope of glory" (Col 1:27). We become attuned to Christ in the sacraments and in contemplative prayer. We learn the way of the Spirit through listening, silence, and the opening of the heart, so that we fulfill the words of the Nicene Creed, "I believe in all that is, seen and unseen."

St. Paul goes further, to tell us about this unveiling: "And we all, who with unveiled faces contemplate the Lord's glory, are being transformed into his image with ever-increasing glory, which comes from the Lord, who is the Spirit" (2 Cor 3:18). This is the amazing hope of such prayer, not simply to connect with God, but to be transformed into the very image of Christ, to become a window into the unseen world of God, and a picture of God's transforming power.

So what is Christianity all about, and what is prayer for the Christian? The answer again comes from the Scriptures, as Jesus engages the disciples of John the Baptist:

> *The next day John was there again with two of his disciples. When he saw Jesus passing by, he said, "Look, the Lamb of God!"*
>
> *When the two disciples heard him say this, they followed Jesus. Turning around, Jesus saw them following and asked, "What do you want?"*
>
> *They said, "Rabbi" (which means "Teacher"), "where are you staying?"*
>
> *"Come," he replied, "and you will see."*
>
> *So they went and saw where he was staying, and they spent that day with him.*
>
> (John 1:35–39 NIV)

Contemplative prayer is the entrance into the place of Jesus—his mind, his vision, his understanding. It is becoming one with Jesus, but not the Jesus that we think we already understand.

Foreword

We are like the disciples of John, who find themselves speaking with Jesus, and spending time with him. And this is what we offer the world, as it roils in its skepticism of Christian faith. As the church struggles to maintain its credibility among sophisticated and educated young adults, especially in the countries where Christianity previously grew and was well established, it is forced to turn back to the ancient Christian message of embracing Jesus as Savior and Teacher. But in our day this embrace is not simply baptism and catechism. Instead, it is the discipline and adventure of prayer—contemplative prayer. The great theologian of Vatican II, Karl Rahner, said it well: "The Christian of the future will be a mystic or he will not exist at all."[2]

Father Larry Hart has described the story of contemplative prayer throughout the history of the 2,000 years of Christian faith, and even long before its appearance. Contemplative prayer is a daunting term for many, but it need not be. It need not be a convoluted system of ranks and stages, unless one is systematically analyzing its psychology in the consciousness of those devoted to it. Instead, the term "contemplative prayer" describes a picture of the forms and discoveries of devotion, with its many teachers and commentators. This is the subject of Larry Hart's present work—what is learned and taught about such practice over the centuries. Many have written about contemplative prayer. It is a formidable task to begin to read the many works of Hebrew, Jewish, and Christian writers from Asia, Europe, and the Western Hemisphere. Here, Larry gives us a concise summary of its history from the times of prehistory all the way to the present age. Such an overview concludes with the place of contemplative prayer in the life of Christians, everyday Christians who work, raise children, pay bills, and who open their hearts to God—sometimes in pain, and sometimes in joy.

But Father Larry writes not simply as a scholar of contemplative prayer, but also as a devotee. He mirrors the teaching of M. Robert Mulholland—whom he quotes in the very first chapter—that one can read the Scriptures for information or transformation.

2. Egan, *Karl Rahner*, 56.

Foreword

So too, one can study the history of prayer and its commentators out of curiosity and a desire for historical information on the growth of its practice; or one can study its history to reflect upon the place and power of prayer in one's own life.

For the devout Christian who studies such history, the latter is essential, for it is the path of discovery, over mountain and valley, which arrives at peace—the path of the Lord Jesus Christ. He affirmed this path of devotion, after dying and rising, by appearing to his disciples and breathing the Spirit upon them, with these words: "Peace be with you" (John 20:21).

Fr. James Farris
Laguna Beach, Pentecost 2018

Introduction

> In the strict sense of the word, contemplation is a supernatural love and knowledge of God, simple and obscure, infused by him into the summit of the soul, giving it direct and experimental contact with Him. Mystical contemplation is an intuition of God born of pure love.[3]
>
> Thomas Merton

> There are so many Christians who do not appreciate the magnificent dignity of their vocation to sanctity, to the knowledge, love and service of God. There are so many Christians who do not realize what possibilities God has placed in the life of the Christian—what possibilities for joy and love of Him. There are so many Christians who have practically no idea of the immense love of God for them, and of the power of that love to do them good, to bring them happiness.[4]
>
> Thomas Merton

DEEP CALLING TO DEEP

CONTEMPLATIVE PRAYER IS OPENING ourselves to the presence of the mystery of God. Contemplative prayer is deep listening—"deep calling to deep" (Ps 42:7). Without this deep listening, *ennui*

---

3. Merton, *What is Contemplation?*, 36.
4. Ibid., 7.

Introduction

and banality slowly enshroud the spiritual life of the individual Christian man or woman like some ominous fog, and the church as a whole becomes frivolous, irrelevant, inconsequential. It may be as Thomas Merton noted that not everyone is called to be a contemplative in the strict sense, but prayer with at least a contemplative element or orientation to it is the vocation of every disciple—ancient and modern. "Real contemplatives," Merton thought, "will always be rare and few. But that is not a matter of importance as long as the whole church is predominantly contemplative in all her teaching, in all her activity and all her prayer."[5]

CONTEMPLATION AND THE SACRA PAGINA

When Scripture is studied without contemplation the result is sterility—an exercise in mere academic curiosity. There is a vast difference, as M. Robert Mulholland has pointed out, between reading Scripture for "information" and reading it for "transformation."[6] The contemplative attitude is what allows the scholar, in the midst of rigorous research, to relinquish all attempts to master and control the text—to receive Scripture as having that cherished significance that has the power to alter human destiny. Paul Ricoeur insisted that the only way to get "near to what the text says" is to "live in the *aura* of the very meaning inquired after."[7] It is most certainly possible to study, and to teach, Scripture as one would any secular literature. One can be a biblical scholar in the same way one can be, say, a Chaucerian scholar. But one can become a saint or mystic only through a contemplative reading of the sacred text. St. Thomas Aquinas furnishes us with a beautiful paradigm for serious biblical study. It is said that he wrote his *Summa Theologiae* on his knees so that his scholarly work would also be an act of prayer. To every pastor, priest, preacher, and lay leader or Christian worker, whose desire, in the language of St.

---

5. Ibid., 115.
6. Mulholland, *Shaped By the Word*, 25–30.
7. Ricoeur, *Symbolism of Evil*, 351.

Introduction

Paul to Timothy, is to rightly "handle the word,"[8] it can only be said that it is in the silence and solitude of meditation that we learn the sort of love and humility that introduces the soul to the wisdom of the Word.

A CHURCH NOURISHED BY CONTEMPLATION

Furthermore, without a contemplative orientation, the church becomes part of the social, political, and economic *status quo* so that it supports the systemic thoughtlessness, injustice, and violence of the privileged. Thomas Merton perhaps said it best:

> Without the spirit of contemplation in all our worship—that is to say without the adoration and love of God above all, for his own sake, because he is God—the liturgy will not nourish a really Christian apostolate based on Christ's love and carried out in the *Pneuma*. . . . The most important need in the Christian world today is this inner truth nourished by the spirit of contemplation: the praise and love of God, the longing of the coming of Christ, the thirst for the manifestation of God's glory, his truth, his justice, his kingdom in the world. . . . Without contemplation and interior prayers the Church cannot fulfill the mission to transform and save mankind. Without contemplation, she will be reduced to being the servant of cynical and worldly powers, no matter how hard her faithful may protest that they are fighting for the Kingdom of God.[9]

Christians from every denomination and from across the theological spectrum increasingly find themselves wondering whether there is something more to their faith and life than what they have so far experienced, something that speaks to the greater depths of their interior.

I have written this little history of contemplative prayer out of the desire to do whatever I can toward helping the individual

---

8. 2 Tim 2:15.
9. Merton, *Contemplative Prayer*, 115–16.

Introduction

Christian—as well as the church, the community of our faith—appreciate the contemplative tradition and dimension of our spiritual tradition, and to encourage the orientation toward contemplative prayer as our religious heritage; that is, the strengthening and furtherance of our purity of intention and genuineness of love.

THE TRANSFORMING CENTER

Before continuing on it is important that we attempt to see contemplative prayer as one of the recognizable features of mysticism, for to speak of the contemplative life is to speak of the mystical life. The word "mysticism" has been trodden over by many scholars with many obfuscating definitions. The longer my journey has grown, and the nearer the far shore has become, the less interest I have in the study of academic spirituality—a contradiction in terms and a distraction.

Bernard McGinn, perhaps the preeminent Christian scholar in this regard, defines mysticism as "those beliefs and practices of the faith that concern the preparation for, and the consciousness of the direct and transforming presence of God."[10] But as McGinn goes on to note, mysticism is, more than anything else, a way of life—"a journey to God."[11]

Mystics, both ancient and modern, have spoken of their practice and experience as a conscious connection with God, as an awareness of sacred mystery, as contemplation, as an experience of union and communion with God, as the *beatific vision*, bliss, ecstasy, as an unnamable desire which is, paradoxically, an infinitely satisfying longing. Their descriptions pile up all in a jumble, and tumble over one another for the simple reason that they are all attempts to say the unsayable. "Presence," "consciousness," and "encounter," suggests Bernard McGinn, may be the preferable way of describing the aim of mystical practice. This, he says, is because "God does not become present to human consciousness the way

---

10. McGinn, *Essential Writings of Christian Mysticism*, xiv–xviii.
11. McGinn, *Foundations of Mysticism*, xvi.

Introduction

that an object in the concrete world is said to be present. Encountering God is much more like meeting a friend or loved one."[12] Therefore, mysticism says McGinn, is better defined by the word "consciousness" than "experience," in that mysticism is not simply a bundle of unusual sensations, but a way of loving and knowing based on "states of awareness in which God is present as the direct and transforming center of life."[13]

Regarding whether this encounter of the mystic with the mystery of presence is mediated or unmediated, McGinn notes that all mystics make use of prayers, rituals, ceremonies, and meditation in opening themselves to encounters with God so that it can be said that such experiences are mediated; however, the immediacy and directness in such encounters is so intense, and the firsthand quality of such experiences so real, that it is difficult for the mystic to bring him or herself to describe them or to think of them as mediated. Perhaps the best answer to the question of whether mystical experience, or consciousness, is mediated or unmediated is: "Yes."

THE FRUIT OF CONTEMPLATION

Finally, mysticism is a kind of metamorphosis: "I appeal to you therefore, brothers and sisters, by the mercies of God," writes St. Paul in his Epistle to the Romans,

> to present your bodies as a living sacrifice, holy and acceptable to God, which is your spiritual worship. Do not be conformed to this world but be transformed (*metamorphosed*) by the renewing of your minds, so that you may discern what is the will of God—what is good and acceptable and perfect. (Rom 12:1–3 NRSV)

The only test Christianity has ever known for determining the authenticity of mystics, is that of the transformed and transforming

---

12. McGinn, *Essential Writings of Christian Mysticism*, xv.
13. Ibid., xvi.

Introduction

life; that is, the impact of the mystic's practice on her or his own life and on the lives of others.

To speak of the Christian mystic is simply to speak of a man or woman whose interior life and outward behavior has been dramatically changed by the mysterious inner working of the Holy Spirit to which he or she is open and surrendered. St. Paul thought of it as the Spirit producing fruit, natural and organic, in our lives (Gal 5:22 NASB). Eugene Peterson's rendering of Galatians 5:22–24 contributes profoundly to praying that text contemplatively:

> But what happens when we live God's way (live open and receptive to the Spirit)? God brings gifts into our lives, much the same way that fruit appears in an orchard—things like affection for others, exuberance about life, serenity. We develop a willingness to stick with things, a sense of compassion in the heart, and a conviction that a basic holiness permeates things and people. We find ourselves involved in loyal commitments, not needing to force our way in life, able to marshal and direct our energies wisely.
>
> (Gal 5:22–24 MSG)

Contemplation is welcoming the Spirit, working through Holy Scripture, to do its silent transformative work in us (Eph 6:17; Heb 4:12).

CLARIFYING PROBLEMATIC TERMS

This means that true Christian contemplation is never separate and apart from, or contradictory to, Scripture, which is itself subtle, deep, and mysterious. Rather, meditation enables the reality of Scripture to grow its roots ever deeper within us. Across decades, the words of W. E. Sangster, the great British evangelical Methodist, have stayed with me. Sangster said something to the effect that: "*The most sublime moments of the religious life are those in which we come to know in our heart what we may have understood in our mind all along.*" Christian mysticism tends toward an ever deepening appreciation and appropriation of what has been revealed— for

Introduction

the historic and ecumenical faith. Pseudocontemplation tends toward esoteric intellectualizations and strange inventions. This is one reason we see the endless proliferation of spiritualties in our postmodern world. However, just because the forest is dense, does not mean it is magical.

Karl Rahner, a Jesuit priest and one of the most significant theologians of the twentieth century, thought the term "mysticism" ought to be avoided all together. He thought its association with bizarre psychic phenomena, odd ideas, idiosyncratic philosophies, and its disconnectedness from the normal Christian life, what he called "everyday Christian mysticism,"[14] made it a problematic term. However, Rahner not only used the word, but was himself a profound contemplative and genuine Christian mystic. In the end he was far more concerned with experiencing the reality of God, and consciousness of Christ's living presence, than with the word used to describe that awareness or experience.

INHERENT MYSTERY

When I assert the ubiquitous practice of contemplation in Holy Scripture, I obviously do not mean to suggest it has always been embraced by institutional Judaism or establishment Christendom. Rather, it has been my intention to demonstrate that there have always been individuals and communities within the tradition of historic Christian orthodoxy, and even antecedent to the Hebrew national faith born on Mount Sinai, in which men and women have practiced contemplative prayer. It also means that the practice of contemplative prayer as the presence of God—which is the very definition of mysticism in the Judeo-Christian tradition—is there in the writings which are sacred to the Christian faith, from the opening of Genesis to the concluding words of Revelation. Indeed, it is the thesis here that even the simplest of prayers, if prayed deeply, become contemplative and carry the devotee into what can only properly be called Christian mysticism. Basic to this little

---

14. Egan, *Karl Rahner*, 57.

Introduction

history of contemplation then is the premise that the Christian religion, regardless of how its adherents have frequently abused or distorted the word, is inherently mystical in that it represents the quest for that mysterious and transcendent "something more" to life for which every human heart longs.

ONE

The Invention of Contemplative Prayer: The Stone Age

What then is prayer? . . . Let us begin with one simple fact, so often regarded as a spiritual cliché that we tend to pass too lightly over it. Prayer is the opening of the heart to God.

KARL RAHNER IN *ON PRAYER*[1]

The wonderful beauty of prayer is that the opening of our heart is as natural as the opening of a flower. To let a flower open and bloom it is only necessary to let it be; so, if we simply are, if we become and remain still and silent, our heart cannot but be open, the Spirit cannot but pour through into our whole being. It is for this we have been created.

JOHN MAIN IN *MONASTERY WITHOUT WALLS*[2]

---

1. Rahner, *On Prayer*, 10.
2. Main, *Monastery Without Walls*, 49.

PRIMORDIAL PRAYER

I SOMETIMES WONDER WHO invented prayer. I mean the prayer of the open heart, contemplative prayer, prayer as meditation. Prayer that is wordless and imageless. Prayer as simple being—being in the presence of divine mystery. Prayer as being in love, being in the love of God. Such prayer is, of course, older than the birth of the church, more ancient than Judaism, or the great matriarchs and patriarchs of Holy Scripture. And contrary to popular opinion, it did not originate with Hinduism or Buddhism, but is older than both. The answer to the question is really that no one had to invent meditation or work out a system for contemplative prayer, for it is as natural to being human as affection. No one invented contemplative or meditative prayer; rather it has been discovered in many times, in many places, and by many people of many faiths from the Stone Age to now. Bernard McGinn notes in the first volume of his *The Presence of God: A History of Christian Mysticism*, "It is important to remember mysticism is always a process or way of life."[3] This is no less true of contemplative prayer itself as a specific element of ancient Hebrew spiritual consciousness, and of Christian mysticism from the first century CE to the contemporary practice of the presence of God.[4]

Many anthropologists believe that Paleolithic men and women simply entered a contemplative or meditative state as they sat around the fire, maybe at the entrance to a cave, staring silently, gazing quietly into its burning embers and flames. In time, various meditative practices were developed and employed in all the world religions and wisdom traditions. Bede Griffiths, the modern Benedictine monk and Christian mystic, pointed to awareness of the Holy Trinity as a primordial and continuing experience discovered in walking the contemplative path.[5] If, as more and more scientists are beginning to suspect, we are somehow hardwired for

---

3. McGinn, *Foundations of Mysticism*, xvi.
4. Ibid., xvii.
5. Teasdale, *Bede Griffiths*, 118.

The Invention of Contemplative Prayer: The Stone Age

God, then none of this should in any way be surprising.[6] Our longing for some transcendent something more, for the experience of the divine, is in our very genetics. The saying of St. Augustine that we are made for God and our hearts are always restless until we find our rest in God is evidently true in more ways than Augustine imagined.[7]

The highly regarded Catholic scholar, priest, theologian, and mystic, Karl Rahner, said that the most human of all activities is our response—positive or negative—to the continuous offering of God's own self to each of us in love. To participate in the Easter faith, in the death of Christ, is to die to self and to the world in order to say "Yes" to God's eternal "Yes"—"to surrender to the mystery that permeates daily life." This is that biblical and christological foundation of grace which is at the very heart of human existence, and which renders it impossible to understand the human person as other than *homo mysticus*, "mystical man." Mysticism is nothing less than the experience of this grace, this gift of loving presence, insofar as it can be called an experience, and contemplation being joyfully awake to it in everyday life.[8]

LIFE IS ENCOUNTER

The great Jewish philosopher and theologian Martin Buber said, "All actual life is encounter."[9] By this, Buber meant not only the encounter or meeting of actual persons, but also the possibility of an encounter and of "a mysterious approach to closeness" with the whole of life and reality.[10] "When you consecrate life," he said, "you encounter the living God."[11] In the enormous beauty we see in everything around us we behold the face of God. Consequently,

---

6. Hamer, *God Gene*.
7. Augustine, *Confessions*, 1.
8. Egan, *Rahner*, ch. 3.
9. Ibid., 62.
10. Ibid., 57–58.
11. Ibid., 128.

Buber could illustrate his concept of "I and Thou" with the analogy of contemplating a tree:

> I contemplate a tree. I can accept it as a picture of rigid pillar in a flood of light, of splashes of green traversed by the gentleness of blue silver ground... I can assign it to a species and observe it as an instance, with an eye to its construction and its way of life. I can overcome its uniqueness and form so rigorously that I recognize it only as an expression of the law—those laws according to which a constant opposition of forces is continually adjusted, or those laws according to which the elements mix and separate. I can dissolve it into a number, to a relation between numbers and eternalize it. Throughout all this the tree remains an object and has its place and its time span, its time and condition. But it can also happen, if will and grace are joined, that as I contemplate the tree I am drawn into a relation, and the tree ceases to be an It.[12]

I suspect, although I know of no way to prove it, that something like all of this was involved in the primordial origins of contemplative prayer.

My guess is that the hypothesis of God and human spirituality did not originate as some sort of Freudian wish fulfillment, or as an explanation of some natural phenomenon puzzled out by Lucy, but rather as that inborn awareness, or at least the capacity for that awareness, of the numinous, of divine mystery, of God that is in the very structure of our DNA. For centuries this innate consciousness has been known as the *sensus divinitatis*—the sense of the divine. What I am suggesting is that contemplation is, at the very least, the natural working of the *sensus divinitatis*—a faculty that, like memory, reason, or perception, can lead us into a real knowledge of significant truth and meaning.[13]

---

12. Ibid., 57–58.

13. Plantinga, *Warranted Christian Belief*, 130–32, 139, 148, 172–86, 199, 205, 214–16, 240–46, 280–81, 305, 330–35, 343, 347, 453, 455, 484, 487, 490–92.

The Invention of Contemplative Prayer: The Stone Age

Contemplative prayer is organic, natural, living. And that God would communicate with us through our biochemical processes is entirely reasonable, and even somewhat commmonplace, to anyone familiar with the classical Jewish and Christian understanding of human nature in which the person is understood as an example of psychosomatic unity, rather than as a collection of disparate parts (mind, body, soul, spirit, heart) loosely held together by some sort of invisible Velcro.[14]

THE ONLY GOD WORTH THINKING ABOUT IS BEYOND THOUGHT

One thing this heading means is that there is more of an answer than one might expect to the often-asked question, "If God is really there, then why is that not made plain?" And the answer is that God is manifest to the *sensus divinitatis*—visible in contemplative prayer. The anonymous fourteenth-century author of *The Cloud of Unknowing* was not just writing spiritual fantasy when he said:

> And so diligently persevere until you feel joy in contemplation. For in the beginning it is usual to feel nothing but a kind of darkness about your mind, or as it were a cloud of unknowing. You will seem to know nothing and feel nothing except a naked intent toward God in the depths of your being. Try as you might, this darkness and this cloud will remain between you and God. You will feel frustrated, for your mind will be unable to grasp him, and your heart will not relish the delight of his love. But learn to be at home in this darkness. Return to it as often as you can, letting your spirit cry out to him whom you love. For if, in this life, you hope to find and see God as he is in himself it must be within this darkness and this cloud. But if you strive to fix your love on him forgetting all else, which is the work of contemplation I have urged you to begin, I am confident that God in his goodness will bring you to a deep experience of himself.[15]

14. Sapp, *Sexuality, the Bible, and Science*, 5.
15. Anonymous, *Cloud of Unknowing*, 49.

Again and again the author of the *Cloud of Unknowing* asserts that one can think and reason all one wants, but in the end will inevitably come to something with which the intellect cannot deal. It is difficult, therefore, to imagine that contemplative prayer could have been born in the thinking discursive mind.

CONSECRATE YOUR HEART TO SEE GOD IN ALL THINGS

What I am suggesting is that the primitive practice of identifying trees and fields and rivers and seas with deities may have been primitive only in time, that it may very well have resulted from experiencing the natural world in Buber's sense of encounter and in recognizing the divine in all things. "When you consecrate life you see God"—contemplation, *sensus divinitatis*.

I grew up, in so far as I grew to adulthood in the church, in a very conservative denomination that was suspicious of religious experiences. The legitimacy of any experience was judged on the basis of the obedience which necessarily preceded it. One might, for example, experience a feeling of joy, but that joy was always understood and legitimized by a prior act of obedience. This had the obvious result of numbing spiritual sensitivity and the deep emotions of the interior life. What we learned to do was to focus on inflexibly following the rules, as if we were anxiously fixated on some giant but invisible scoreboard that told us we were behind in points and the outcome of the game did not look good. Even after I had dismissed such ideas as incompatible with life and spiritual reality, and with Scripture itself, I still had the strange notion that only people who were deeply serious about practicing the faith had religious or spiritual experiences.

I refer to this as a strange notion because it does not fit with my own personal life experience. I have had mystical experiences since I was very young that had no necessary connection with religious practices or with being terribly obedient. Years ago, I discovered a question used by the Quakers that is helpful in spiritual formation groups: "When if ever did God become more than just

The Invention of Contemplative Prayer: The Stone Age

a word for you?" I have usually answered that question for myself something like this:

CHILDHOOD TALES OF THE NUMINOUS

When I was maybe four or five years old, I don't really quite remember now, we went to visit my stepgrandparents, Elmer and Vera Emerson. They lived in a Victorian-style house with a huge living room in which the adults were all talking while my cousin and I played. My grandmother, whom people described as an angel, was in a losing battle with breast cancer. She was often in excruciating pain. When the pain became unbearably intense she could go into her bedroom and pray, and when she came out she would be free of the pain—at least for a while. I don't know for sure now, but I think that is probably what the adults were talking about when someone said, "God is everywhere, even in this very room." My cousin and I heard that and got really silly with it. We ran around the room laughing, flailing at the air, and shouting: "Where are you God? I can't see you God! I can't feel you!" My mother stopped us, and very gently, but firmly said something like this, "You can't see God with your eyes or feel God with your hands, but God is here. God is everywhere, and very real. As real as you are. There is nothing greater, or more loving than God and so you should never be silly or disrespectful toward God. And if you remember that God is always with you, even in really bad, scary, sad, or lonely places you will feel better." I was filled with a sense of the immensity, the reality, the vastness, and the closeness of God. And that is the day that God became more than just a word to me. Now, contemplative prayer did not produce that childhood experience, although it was indeed a mystical experience. What contemplation has done is to provide a way of nurturing that experience, of helping me to pay attention, and of understanding and feeling it at an ever deeper level.

    I sometimes tell people a boyhood friend, Kenney Witt, taught me to pray. His last name wasn't really Witt, but his mother would leave him for long periods of time with Old Man Witt, who lived farther down from us on a little country road in a small green ramshackle house hidden among giant cottonwood trees. He was a somewhat disreputable character. He was the last working blacksmith in Kern County, and was as tough as he was old. But he knew a lot about the Bible—most of which he ignored. Kenney was a lost little boy. My sister didn't like Kenny. She said he was like some furtive wild animal. So she didn't trust him. But he was my friend. We spent many hours together especially in the summers. The climate has changed in Bakersfield since I was a kid. Back then there were long stretches in the summer where it was over 110 degrees every day. Frequently, my mother would let us sleep out on the lawn in the hot summer night. One night, Kenney and I were lying on the pile of quilts we had spread on the soft green grass for a bed, looking into the starry night—so many stars. The surpise and wonder of stars shooting across the heavens. And, Kenney, after it had been quiet for some time, said: "Do you pray?" I answered with a strange question, "How do you pray?" "Well," explained Kenney, "I pray like this: 'Now as they lay me down to sleep, I pray the Lord my soul to keep. If I should die before I wake, I pray the Lord my soul to take.' Then I say," he went on, "'God bless Mom, God bless Dad (that's what he called the old man) God bless Rex (the scary German Shepherd), and God bless the whole world.' And then I go to sleep." For many years after that night I prayed the prayer poor little Kenney taught me. And to this day when I hear it lampooned I do not laugh. What I am suggesting is that even a simple child's prayer may be contemplative, is contemplative, if it helps two little lost boys staring into the starry night see God in its immense beauty and wonder. For contemplative prayer is as natural as the innocence of childhood, and its practice nurtures and enriches the magic of every mystical moment, not so much across great reaches of time, but in a way that transcends time.

ALL EARTH IS CRAMMED WITH HEAVEN

What I know now is that everyone, except perhaps a very few suffering from some serious psychopathology such as a Sociopathic

The Invention of Contemplative Prayer: The Stone Age

Personality Disorder, has mystical, religious, or spiritual experiences. I love the lines from Elizabeth Barrett Browning's poem "Aurora Leigh":

> Earth's crammed with heaven,
> And every common bush afire with God;
> But only those who see take off their shoes,
> The rest sit round it and pluck blackberries.[16]

The question is not whether we have spiritual experiences, but whether we are aware of them—whether we are awake or asleep.

So which of our experiences are spiritual in nature rather than mundane, ordinary, without depth of meaning or mystical significance? I am not, of course, actually asking you to categorize your experiences in this way, but rather hoping that by asking this question you will see and grasp the obvious—that all experiences are spiritual, and that the real issue is whether we recognize them as such. Everything that happens—everything you think, say, feel, or do, everything that touches you, no matter how lightly or subtly—is a spiritual experience. Most people, most of the time, do unconsciously sort their experiences into various categories—physical, intellectual, emotional or psychological, spiritual or religious. Often this is helpful in that it makes it possible for us to look at some specific aspect of our life that we need to examine more closely. But it also frequently blunts our spiritual awareness so that we are like the fish that swims everywhere looking for that mysterious and wonderful thing called water.

Over time, the practice of contemplation ought to increase our awareness of the spiritual mystery in which, like the fish in water, "we live, move, and have our very being."[17] It should heighten our consciousness of God at all times, in all places, and in all things, both great and small, as the reality in which we are saturated. Inherent in the practice of contemplation is gratitude. Without gratitude there is no contemplation. We see God in the small, ordinary, events in which our lives are immersed through the cultivation of

---

16. Browning, *Aurora Leigh*, 307.
17. Acts 17:28.

gratitude which is simply another way of speaking of the practice of contemplation. For both gratitude and contemplation involve a kind of openness and receptivity.

There are four lines from William Blake's "Auguries of Innocence" that point in this very direction and make a wonderful meditation:

> To see a world in a grain of sand
> And a heaven in a wild flower
> Hold infinity in the palm of your hand
> And eternity in an hour.[18]

But how does one "hold infinity in the palm of the hand," or "eternity in an hour?" I believe that it is possible to do so through a nonanalytical appreciation of absolutely everything, a gentle awareness, a clear consciousness of what is, through the faculty of uncomplicated intuition, quiet receptivity, and a thankful spirit—that is, through contemplation.

In one of his poems, W. B. Yeats imagines a fifty-year-old man sitting alone at a little marble-topped table in a crowded shop with a book and a now-empty cup. It is an entirely simple and common scene. As he watches all the ordinary people in the shop and on the street, he experiences an extraordinary and profound sense of gratitude, a sense of having been blessed, and of desiring to bless:

> My fiftieth year had come and gone,
> I sat, a solitary man,
> In a crowded London shop,
> An open book and empty cup
> On the marble table top,
> While on the shop and street I gazed
> My body of a sudden blazed;
> And twenty minutes more or less
> It seemed so great my happiness,
> That I was blessed and could bless.[19]

---

18. Blake, "Auguries of Innocence," 86.
19. Yeats, "Vacillation," 135.

The Invention of Contemplative Prayer: The Stone Age

Is Yeats attempting to remind us of that modest altar—that common chalice drained to the bottom by earthly men and women, celebrating the plainest of meals—to the unpretentious words of that simple book venerated by Christians? I think he is. I think he is alluding to the unassuming and therefore most essential realities of Holy Communion.

I find this a profoundly contemplative poem. It makes me think of that scene in Marilynne Robinson's book, *Gilead*, where John recalls how as a young boy he had gone with his father to pull down the remains of a Black Baptist church that had been struck by lightning and burned.[20] It was during a time of adversity in their rural community, everyone was poor, and now this church had burned. As they worked at pulling down the charred remains and clearing away the sooty debris, it began to rain, but still they all sang as they labored. They sang "The Old Rugged Cross," and "Blessed Jesus." "The ashes turned liquid in the rain and the men who were working in the rain got entirely black and filthy, till you could hardly tell one from another."[21] John remembers his father down on his heels in the rain, water dripping from his hat, feeding him an ashy biscuit from scorched hands. For John this becomes a moment of Holy Eucharist. He thinks of a phrase often used in those days—"the bread of affliction." As John's work-worn father breaks the ashy biscuit in two and gives John half, it is, for John, a "visionary" moment in which he "comprehends his life."[22] Can you taste the grace and love of communion in a piece of broken bread, or comprehend your life in a little sip of wine?

SEEING WITH THE EYES OF LOVE

Gerald May—psychiatrist, author, and spiritual director—wrote something in his book, *The Awakened Heart*, that is pertinent to

---

20. Robinson, *Gilead*, 94–96.
21. Ibid., 117.
22. Ibid., 116, 118.

the origins and practice of contemplative prayer, and which I find myself returning to again and again. May wrote:

> There is a desire within each of us, in the deep center of ourselves that we call our heart. We were born with it, it is never completely satisfied, and it never dies. We are often unaware of it, but it is always awake. It is the human desire for love. Every person yearns to love, to be loved, to know love. Our true identity, our reason for being, is to be found in this desire.... In most of us the desire for love has often been distorted or buried, but if you look at your own life with honest and gentle eyes, you can discern it in yourself as a deep seeking of connectedness, healing, creation, and joy. This is your true identity; it is who you really are, and what you exist for. You have your own unique experience of desiring love, but there is something universal about it as well; it connects you with all other human beings and with all of creation. It is possible to run away from the desire for years, even decades, at a time, but we cannot eradicate it entirely. It keeps touching us in little glimpses and hints in our dreams, our hopes, our unguarded moments. We may go to sleep, but our desire for love does not. It is who we are.[23]

What May writes is entirely biblical, and could have easily been ended with numerous Scripture citations in parentheses. "God is love," says 1 John 4:8b. Of course, this is not the same, as May later points out, as saying "Love is God." To say the latter would be an idolatrous affirmation, for it would be to make a quality of God ultimate, or to deify our own idea of what love is. But we are confident, as the sacred text makes clear, that we were made in love, for love, and by love. The two great precepts of Christianity are that we love God with our whole being, and that we love those around us in the same way we have been loved by Christ. And, in the apostle Paul's correspondence with the Corinthians, we learn that love is itself a way of knowledge and wisdom. God is mystery, everyone you meet is mystery, you are mystery, and there are things about God, about you, and about everyone you meet, that

---

23. May, *Awakened Heart*, 1–3.

The Invention of Contemplative Prayer: The Stone Age

can only be fathomed by love. Yes, what May writes is a marvelous description of contemplation, simple and natural. Contemplation is to see with the eyes of love, and to see with the eyes of love is as organic as it is to see with our physical eyes.

We can sum up, then, the origins and practice of contemplative prayer like this: There is nothing simpler or truer to original pristine creation than love when it is pure. Didn't Jesus say, "How happy are those with a pure heart, for they shall see God?"[24]

---

24. Matt 5:8.

TWO

Contemplative Prayer and the Old Testament

The self is not the hub, but the spoke of the revolving wheel. In prayer we shift the center of living from self-consciousness to self-surrender. God is the center toward which all forces tend. He is the source and we are the flowing of his force, the ebb and flow of His tides.

ABRAHAM JOSHUA HESCHEL IN *QUEST FOR GOD*[1]

To pray is to take notice of the wonder, to regain a sense of the mystery that animates all beings, the divine margin in all attainments. Prayer is our humble answer to the inconceivable surprise of living.

ABRAHAM JOSHUA HESCHEL IN *QUEST FOR GOD*[2]

---

1. Heschel, *Quest for God*, 7.
2. Ibid., 5.

Contemplative Prayer and the Old Testament

METAPHOR OF THE TREE

WHAT I AM CONCERNED with, as someone within the Judeo-Christian tradition, is how this apparently natural phenomenon of contemplative prayer and consciousness has manifested itself in the Hebrew and Christian faiths. Biblically the idea is present from the very beginning. It is there in Genesis and runs all the way through to the end of Revelation.[3]

In the beginning, Genesis says, God created a garden with every pleasing tree as a home for Adam and Eve. After eating the forbidden fruit, Adam and Eve hide from God when "they hear the sound of the Lord walking in the cool of the day" (Gen 2:8; 3:8). In ancient Persia, when the king wanted to honor someone he might make that person "a companion of the garden." This meant that this individual had the privilege of being in the presence of the king as they strolled through the royal gardens, sometimes silently, wordlessly, and at others conversing intimately. The description of God as walking, moving in the garden in the cool of the day is a wonderful metaphor for being peacefully with God—moving with God in quiet harmony.

It is informative that the word for "tree" in Genesis 2:5; 3:4 also means to "meditate." The connotation is of upward motion, and therefore can be used spiritually with regard to growth or elevation. Tree symbolism is important in Scripture as a way of suggesting the whole array of meditative methods for communing with the transcendental.[4]

BY WAY OF BEER LACHAI ROI

The first specific reference in the Bible to meditation is in Genesis 24:62. Rebekah has just been brought back to marry Isaac, and right before they meet, the text says: "Isaac came from the way of Beer Lachai Roi . . . and Isaac went out to meditate (*suach*) in the

---

3. Kaplan, *Bible and Meditation*. Also see: Eaton, *Contemplative Face of Old Testament Wisdom*.

4. Kaplan, *Bible and Meditation*, 106–7.

field toward evening." The word *suach* occurs only this one time in the Bible, and means some type of prayer. Aryeh Kaplan quotes those Jewish commentators who believe that Isaac was engaged in a classical form of meditation. Beer Lachai Roi was considered a holy place since it was here that the angel had appeared to Hagar, and so is the place Isaac went each afternoon to practice "the inner isolation of meditation."[5]

The word *suach* is closely related to the word *siyach*, and its derivative *sichah*, which occurs more frequently, as in:

> I recall my melody at night, I meditate (*siyach*) with my heart and my spirit (*ruach*) seeks. (Ps 77:7)[6]

Siyach can also refer to chanting and singing:

> I will sing to God with my life, I will chant to my God with my existence, let my meditation (*siyach*) be sweet to Him, I will rejoice in God. (Ps 104:33–34)[7]

Kaplan writes,

> *Siyach* therefore refers to speech that is not uttered for its own sake, but in order to remove other thoughts from the mind, clearing it of other mundane ideas. Its main connotation is therefore that of distraction, being a process intended to *remove* all extraneous thoughts from the mind (italics his).[8]

The concept of *Siyach* is, consequently, closely linked to the quest for enlightenment, and to exploring the deeper questions of reality and existence with one's *ruach*-spirit.[9]

---

5. Ibid., 101–2.
6. Ibid., 102.
7. Ibid., 103.
8. Ibid., 104.
9. Ibid., 102–5.

Contemplative Prayer and the Old Testament

THE PROPHET AS MYSTIC

Nearly everyone who has studied the Old Testament at all knows of the prophets' passion for justice, and their courage in confronting social evils, such as the exploitation of the poor and vulnerable by the wealthy elite. However, what few people realize is that the prophets also represented one of the great mystical traditions of the world. The Hebrew prophets practiced various forms of deep meditation; empty of ego and blind self-will, they were open and receptive to divine presence and mystery.

Those who sought to prepare themselves for prophetic ministry were known as "the sons of the prophets," and normally spent years in intense training and spiritual discipline. The difference between the Old Testament prophets and other mystics is that the prophets were more specific and clear in their messages. "The true prophet," says Kaplan, "is able to channel this spiritual power, focusing it clearly enough to obtain an unambiguous message."[10]

QUIETING THE MUTINY

Three other words from the root *Hagha* offer further evidence of meditative or contemplative prayer as a spiritual practice in ancient Israel. *Hagha* is related to thought:

> May the words of my mouth, and the meditation (*hagayon*) of my heart, be acceptable to You, O God. (Ps 19:15)

Hagha can create some confusion in that it can carry the connotation of both speech and thought. However, it can also mean an inarticulate and repetitive sound such as an animal makes. For example, "I will coo (*hagah*) like a dove," (Isa 38:14) or "growl (*hagah*) like a lion over its prey" (Isa 31:4). It can also denote a gasp: "Our days end as a gasp (*hegeh*)."[11] Or, "They make no sound with their throat" (Ps 115:7). The root *Hagah*, therefore, has to do with a sound or thought that can be repeated over and over like the

---

10. Ibid., 30.
11. Ibid., 111–12.

cooing of a dove or the growling of a lion. In Psalms 92:3 and 4, it is associated with music: "To speak of Your love in the morning, and Your faith by night; with a ten stringer, with a lute, with meditation (*higayon*) on the harp." *Higayon*, then, can refer to the repetition of a mantra-like formula, which can even be a set of notes or a melody repeated on a lute or harp or some other instrument. "*Hagah* taken with the connotation of purification would signify the clearing of the mind in order to direct it to one goal."[12] Kaplan goes on to note that Plato likened the discipline of the mind to the steering of a ship:

> The human mind is very much like a ship where the sailors have mutinied and have locked the captain and navigator in the cabin. Each sailor believes himself free to steer the ship as he pleases. First one sailor, and then another, takes the helm, while the ship travels on a random and erratic course. These sailors cannot agree on a goal, and even if they could, they do not know how to navigate the ship to reach it. The task of the individual is to quell the mutiny and to release the navigator and captain. Only then is he or she free to choose a goal and steer a straight course to reach it. The biblical word *Hagah* appears to denote a similar idea. One must put aside and remove all mutinous thoughts and allow the ship of the mind to be steered in a constant and consistent direction toward a well-defined goal.[13]

It is of further informative interest to note here that the Hebrew word *Hegeh*, meaning "rudder" or "helm," has exactly the same root letters as *Hegah*, meaning "meditation."

To meditate is to provide the mind with a rudder and helm. Kaplan continues:

> It is in this sense that *Hagah* means to repeat something over and over, periodically and cyclically, as in mantra

---

12. Ibid., 111–13.
13. Ibid., 113–14.

Contemplative Prayer and the Old Testament

meditation. It is the direction of the mind that comes through such constant repetition.[14]

As Kaplan therefore understands the term,

> *Hagah* refers to a process that brings the mind to a state where it is devoid of all activity. The mind thus reaches a level where it is empty of everything other than pure, simple, and elemental existence.[15]

THE HEBREW SAGES

Where Kaplan is primarily interested in the mystical and meditative practices of the prophets, John Eaton, Reader in Old Testament Studies in the University of Birmingham, England, focuses on the contemplative spirituality and wisdom of the Old Testament sages. Eaton correctly observes that attentiveness is an essential characteristic of all contemplation. When offered whatever gift he might desire, Solomon asked only for (*leb shome*) the heart that hears (1 Kgs 3:9). Eaton writes:

> Prominent in the opening chapters of Proverbs are the calls to the disciple for openness and attention: "Hear. . . turn. . . receive. . . be attentive. . . plead for insight. . . seek. . . incline your ear. . . keep your heart with vigilance. . . let not your heart turn aside. . . listen. . . watch. . . wait. . . !" So valuable is attention that it is thought of as fresh from the creator's hand: "A listening ear and a seeing eye, the Lord hath made them both" (Proverbs 20:12).[16]

In many of the Psalms, like Psalms 73 and 119, Eaton sees the evidence of spiritual discipline, of meditative practice, and Psalms 27 as a "striking expression of contemplation":

> The Lord is my light and my salvation,

---

14. Ibid., 114.
15. Ibid., 114.
16. Eaton, *Contemplative Face of Old Testament*, 40.

> Whom shall I fear?
> One thing have I asked of the Lord,
>   that alone I shall seek,
> That I may sit in the house of the Lord
>   all the days of my life,
> To behold the beauty of the Lord
>   and to meditate in his temple.
> Ps 27:1, 4 (NASB)

The highest form of prayer, praise, and communion with God in the Old Testament is silence. Abraham Joshua Heschel, the great Jewish scholar and mystic, said in his book *Quest for God: Studies in Prayer and Symbolism*, "The highest form of worship is that of silence and hope"—of waiting.[17]

> Commune with your hearts and be still. . .
> Ps 4:5

> To Thee silence is praise.
> Ps 65:2

> The Lord is in his Holy Temple;
> Let all the earth keep silence before Him.
> Hab 2:20[18]

God is made known in the Hebrew Scriptures through attentive silence, watchful stillness, calm wakefulness. Twice in Psalm 62 the writer speaks of waiting in silence:

> For God alone my soul waits in silence;
>   from him comes my salvation.
> Psalms 62:1(RSV)

> For God alone my soul waits in silence,
>   for my hope is from him.
> Psalms 62:6 (RSV)

In both cases each line begins with the little word *akh* for which there is no exact English equivalent. It means something like, "I don't care what anyone says, I am sure that. . ." and then follows

---

17. Heschel, *Quest for God*, 41.
18. Ibid., 42.

Contemplative Prayer and the Old Testament

a forceful positive assertion. We might therefore render verses one and six as George Knight does: "Say what you like, but unto God—my whole being—in silence."[19] In the Hebrew there is no verb here. If that seems strange to us then we must remember that it is because this is the grammar of holy mystery.

Eaton says of silence in the wisdom literature, and of how contemplation inevitably leads to silence:

> When all concepts have been denied, the soul becomes completely speechless in union with the Inexpressible. Whether in such mystical depths, or in the general life of humility and attention, the fitness of silence and economy of speech is generally accepted by contemplatives.... Economy of speech was much valued by the Old Testament sages. The wise are pictured as knowing when silence is best and as reflecting before answering.... Let not man multiply words beyond God's, for the human unreliability will soon become apparent. For *Qohelet* it is man's situation in the midst of infinite mystery that makes much talking inappropriate. Why should he hold forth as if he held his destiny in his own hands (Eccles. 6:10f; 10:14; Eccles. 28:25f)?[20]

How does one come to know God in the depths of one's being? Simply by being quiet, silent, still. In the words of Psalms 46:10, "Be still, cease striving, and know that I am God."

Given the frequency with which words for "waiting" occur in the Old Testament, one might well wish that *The Contemplative Face of Old Testament Wisdom* had done more to develop waiting itself as a spiritual practice. In Psalms 62, the tension of waiting is especially apparent. In fact, *Qavah*, "to wait," originally referred to the braided or twisted strands of a cord of rope. It is the tension of not knowing or possessing. It is that quality of detached waiting in receptive love described by the medieval author of *The Cloud of Unknowing*. It is not, as Paul Tillich noted, that the prophets, psalmists, and apostles were waiting merely for the consummation

---

19. Knight, *Daily Study Bible Series*, 285.
20. Eaton, *Contemplative Face of Old Testament*, 58–59.

of history, the end judgment of all things, but instead they were waiting for the God who brings the end. They were waiting for the God who is the fulfillment of all things.[21] Paradoxically, as in inaugural eschatology's "the already and the not yet," the contemplative waits for what already is. The psalmist speaks of waiting for God with one's whole being. Waiting incorporates our yearning for God, as well as the realization that God who is infinite mystery is not a thing to be possessed or controlled by us—not in a doctrine, not in an institution, not in a book, and not within our own experience. To put it simply, there is no better definition of contemplative prayer than the words of Psalms 62, "To God alone, my whole being in silence."

OLD TESTAMENT STORIES OF CONTEMPLATION

What I would suggest at this point is that you reflect on the following stories in light of what has been noted so far and see if you can taste the mystical or the strong contemplative flavor of the Old Testament.[22]

A Sound of Sheer Silence

> At that place he came to a cave, and spent the night there. Then the word of the Lord came to him, saying, "What are you doing here, Elijah?" He answered, "I have been very zealous for the Lord, the God of hosts; for the Israelites have forsaken your covenant, thrown down your altars, and killed your prophets with the sword. I alone am left, and they are seeking my life, to take it away."
>
> He said, "Go out and stand on the mountain before the Lord, for the Lord is about to pass by."
>
> Now there was a great wind, so strong that it was splitting mountains and breaking rocks in pieces before the Lord, but the Lord was not in the wind; and after the wind an earthquake, but the Lord was not in the

---

21. Tillich, *Shaking of the Foundations*, 149–52.
22. Kaplan, *Bible and Meditation*, 44–56.

earthquake; and after the earthquake a fire, but the Lord was not in the fire; and after the fire a sound of sheer silence. When Elijah heard it, he wrapped his face in his mantle and went out and stood at the entrance of the cave. Then there came a voice to him that said, "What are you doing here, Elijah?"

1 Kings 19:9–13 NRSV

Mystery of the Burning Bush

Now Moses was pasturing the flock of Jethro his father-in-law, the priest of Midian; and he led the flock to the west side of the wilderness, and came to Horeb, the mountain of God.

And the angel of the Lord appeared to him in a blazing fire from the midst of a bush; and he looked and behold, the bush was burning with fire, yet the bush was not consumed.

So Moses said, "I must turn aside now and see this marvelous sight, why the bush is not burned up."

When the Lord saw that he turned aside to look, God called to him from the midst of the bush, and said, "Moses, Moses!" And he said, "Here am I."

Then he said, "Do not come near here; remove your sandals from your feet, for the place on which you are standing is holy ground."

He said also, "I am the God of your father, the God of Abraham, the God of Isaac, and the God of Jacob."

Then Moses hid his face, for he was afraid to look at God. And the Lord said, "I have surely seen the affliction of my people who are in Egypt, and have given heed to their cry because of their taskmasters, for I am aware of their sufferings. So I have come to deliver them from the power of the Egyptians, and to bring them up from that land to a good and spacious land . . ."

Then said Moses to God, "Behold I am going to the children of Israel, and I shall say to them, 'The God of your fathers has sent me.' Now they may say to me, 'What is his name?' What shall I say to them?"

> And God said to Moses, "I AM WHO I AM'" and he said, "Thus you shall say to the children of Israel, I Am has sent me to you".
>
> Exodus 3:1–13 NASB

Account of the Chariots

In my thirtieth year, on the fifth day of the fourth month, as one of the displaced Hebrew captives living along the River Chebar in Babylon, the heavens opened and I saw visions of God.

(On the fifth of the month in the fifth year of King Jehoiachin's exile, the word of the Lord came with clarity to Ezekiel the priest, and son of Buzi, by the river Chebar. The Lord's hand was placed on Ezekiel and Ezekiel was given visions.)

And behold, I saw a powerful wind storm coming from the north, a great cloud continually flashing fire, and with a bright dazzling glow all around. And in the center of the cloud and in the midst of the fire a vision of the Chashmal,[23] the speaking silence, shining with a metallic like brilliance.

And in the storm I saw four Chayot—four Living Creatures. This is what they looked like in my vision: They resembled human beings in some ways, but each of them had four faces and four wings. Their legs were like those of a person but the soles of their feet were like a calf's foot and gleamed like polished copper. I could see that beneath each of their wings they had human hands.

The four Living Beings were joined wing to wing, and when they flew they did not turn, but flew straight in whatever direction they intended. Each had a human face in front, a lion's face on the right side, the face of an ox on the left side, and an eagle's face at the back. Spreading out

---

23. The word "chashmal" is used three times in Ezekiel to describe what he saw as the center of the manifestation of God. There is no definitive agreement as to its meaning. It could mean something which shines with dazzling brilliance—amber or glowing metal. The Septuagint renders it as "electrum." It could also be a compound word meaning silence (chash) and speaking(milel); hence, speaking silence.

from the back of each were two pair of wings. One pair of wings connected to the wings of the Living Being on each side and one pair covered their body.
The Chayot ran and returned like bolts of lightning.
. . . whenever they were still they dropped their wings, folding them against their body. I heard a voice from the astonishingly beautiful crystal expanse above them.
Then I saw what appeared to be a throne made of sapphire. Sitting on the throne was a figure in human form. From the waist up it was glowing like iron in the furnace—a vision of the Chashmal, of the Speaking Silence. From the waist down it was like flames of burning fire. Within there was a glow all around the figure. The vision of the halo was like seeing a rainbow in the clouds on a rainy day. This was the vision of God's glory. I saw it and I fell on my face. Then I heard a voice speak.

Ezekiel 1:1–2, 25, 28

SILENT MUSIC

Here in each of these stories is contemplation as mystically understood—being, being here now, attentiveness to divine mystery, listening in sacred stillness, listening for the "speaking silence." It reminds one of the words from a poem by Saint John of the Cross: "My beloved is the mountains, the solitary wooded valleys, strange islands. . . silent music."[24]

---

24. Johnston, *Silent Music*, 6.

THREE

Contemplative Prayer and the New Testament

Christian contemplation is the answer to a call and the response to a vision. One cannot embark on the journey until one has heard the voice and glimpsed the footprints of the ox. In other words there is an initial awakening. One stops in one's tracks amazed by the realization that one is loved. Christian contemplation begins with the belief, the conviction, the experience of God's love for me. It never starts with vigorous efforts on my part; it does not manifest itself through active energy; it does not begin with my violently drumming up some powerful love for God and others. This is stated explicitly by John: "In this is love, not that we loved God but that God loved us" (1 John 4:10).

WILLIAM JOHNSTON IN *SILENT MUSIC*[1]

Prayer is a song that can only be sung to God in the stillness of our hearts.

KARL RAHNER IN *ON PRAYER*[2]

1. Johnston, *Silent Music*, 17.
2. Rahner, *On Prayer*, 60.

Contemplative Prayer and the New Testament

INSTRUCTION IN MYSTICAL PRAYER

THE NEW TESTAMENT ACTUALLY records very little on the methods of prayer of any sort, but all prayer is ultimately mystical. There is, for example, nothing at all like Richard Foster's *Prayer: The Heart's True Home*, Margaret Gunther's *The Practice of Prayer*, or Basil Pennington's book *Centering Prayer*.[3] John Cobb, the process theologian, notes that neither Jesus nor the other authors of the New Testament offer any real instruction in prayer, certainly no systematic or detailed instruction, on the methods of prayer.[4] Cobb is, of course, correct, but that is not as odd as it may seem at first, or as significant as Cobb may think. Myriads and myriads of the things we know, say, and do, both secular and sacred, are derived from the family and culture into which we are born. We don't receive formal instruction on how to talk, we just begin, first with sighs and coos, then babbling, followed soon by individual words, and finally in complete sentences. And we speak the language spoken around us and to us. First-century Palestine, indeed the whole world, was saturated with the mechanics of prayer and religious observances meant to lead to a transformation of consciousness. But the lack of systematic teaching of prayer techniques in the Bible can also be attributed to something else.

We learn to pray by praying. No matter how much we have taken in from our family, church, or culture, the depth and breadth and ways of our praying expand as our practice of prayer expands. I didn't learn contemplative prayer from anyone or by reading a book. I learned it by praying. I had been a pastor in a conservative denomination for eight or nine years, and all prayers—both congregational and individual—were extemporaneous. The ability to pray for a long time without rambling was seen as a mark of one's spiritual depth. In time I became dissatisfied and restless with my own personal prayer life. I didn't see anything amiss with praying extemporaneously; I still pray such prayers today. It was just that I

---

3. Pennington, *Centering Prayer*. Also: Gunther, *Practice of Prayer*. Foster, *Celebration of Discipline*.

4. Cobb, *Jesus' Abba*, 48–49.

felt there had to be more. The first change I made was how I began my prayer time. Before beginning to pray I would sit quietly listening to music—Maranatha or John Michael Talbot. Later I thought of this as part of what Richard Foster meant by "centering down,"[5] or what Judaism means by: "When you pray, know before whom you stand." But at the time, if I had given it a name I probably would have said I was getting set, getting in the mood, to pray. I would read a verse of Scripture and then pray as I always had—words of praise, petition, confession, and gratitude. I might read from something like E. Stanley Jones's *The Way*. As that experience deepened and became more meaningful, I didn't want to rush away from it—haste and hurry work against the spiritual life. And so I would sit still, reflecting for longer and longer periods of time. That is how I learned to meditate or to pray contemplatively. Only later did I discover there were books written by wise and knowledgeable people on what I was experiencing. In fact, you will want to be careful about reading too many books—it can be distracting. And some writers are neither wise nor knowledgeable. Now, your experience will be far different than mine, but we all learn to pray by praying. There is no need to look for an esoteric formula either in Scripture or elsewhere. There is, however, more in the Gospels and in the New Testament concerning contemplative or meditative prayer than we might think.

THE PRACTICE OF JESUS

Both Jesus and his cousin John, who prepares the way for Jesus, are acknowledged as prophets in the Gospels. Priests came from Jerusalem to ask John, who was an ascetic or Nazarite (Matt 3:4; Num 6:1–21), if he was, as many people thought, the Messiah or a kind of Elijah—the great prophet of Israel (John 1:21). Jesus says of John, "He (John) is himself Elijah who was to come" (Matt 11:14; 17:12 NASB). And when Jesus asked his disciples who people thought he (Jesus) was, they replied, ". . . Elijah, others say one of the prophets"

---

5. Foster, *Celebration of Discipline*, 24.

Contemplative Prayer and the New Testament

(Mark 8:28 NASB). The point is that the identification of Jesus and John as prophets like those of old serves to connect them, however indirectly, with the mystical and contemplative practices of the prophets. Jesus' struggle with evil and temptation in the wilderness for forty days is like that of Elijah's in the wilderness and in the mountain cave. There are any number of such links between the two stories.

For the prophets to reach a meditative state involved a cessation of activity. All ego and sensation had to be quieted. The prophet Elisha directed his disciple Gehazi, "If you meet anyone on the way do not stop to greet him, and if anyone greets you, do not answer" (2 Kgs 4:29 NEB).[6] This quieting of the heart and mind and body, this stillness, was both an external and internal practice. Indeed, external solitude is practiced in order to find internal solitude.

The Gospel according to Mark says, "And in the early morning while it was still dark Jesus arose and went out to a lonely place, and was praying there" (Mark 1:35 NASB). Solitude, a central practice of all contemplatives, is obviously an established spiritual discipline of Jesus. Repeatedly we read of Jesus going off to an isolated place to pray. "But Jesus himself," writes Luke, "would often slip away to the wilderness and pray" (Luke 5:16 NASB). Furthermore, this is a practice to which Jesus sought to introduce his disciples:

> And Jesus said to the apostles, "Come away by yourselves to a lonely place and rest a while." (For there were many people coming and going, and they did not even have time to eat.) And they went away in a boat to a lonely place by themselves. (Mark 6:30–32 NASB)

Unfortunately, because of our rather superficial and narcissistic modern reading of Scripture, we miss hearing any indication of spiritual practice in texts like this, and think Jesus and the disciples were merely leaving for a nice vacation on the beach somewhere.

Everywhere we look in the Gospels we see the contemplative wisdom of Jesus. William Johnston, who sees the contemplative

---

6. Kaplan, *Bible and Meditation*, 7.

wisdom of Jesus as synonymous with the mysticism of love, therefore writes:

> Again, if mysticism is the wisdom which comes from divine love, can we not see Jesus as the mystic *par excellence*? Because love for his Father was the dominating passion of his life: "Abba, Father!" And the whole Gospel relates the drama of how Jesus loved the Father, how he was loved by the Father, and how he offered himself for the world, praying for his disciples "that the love with which thou hast loved me may be in them, and I in them" (John 17:26).[7]

In the Gospels there is the contemplative wisdom of the parables and *aphorisms* of Jesus, the mysticism of the present moment as Jesus speaks of a life lived free of anxiety, moments of astonishing enlightenment as Jesus opens the eyes of the blind and announces to the disciples, "Blessed are your eyes because they see" (Matt 13:16). And there are, as cited above, those rhythmic times of Jesus going into the mountains and wilderness to pray in solitude, as was his custom. There are, it is true, no specific descriptions of Jesus' prayer practice at such times, but the signs surely indicate it included what we would acknowledge as contemplative prayer.

JESUS' INSTRUCTION ON HOW TO PRAY

Jesus does, of course, offer the disciples brief instruction on how to pray, an instruction that is particularly pertinent here. Eugene Peterson's version of Matthew 6:5–13 in *The Message* is especially helpful for gaining a more nuanced perspective. What I am going to quote first from Peterson's translation is just the instruction that precedes the prayer itself. Try to notice that while Jesus goes on to provide something of a discursive prayer for the disciples, the instruction itself contains familiar characteristics of contemplative prayer, such as the emphasis on solitude, honesty, simplicity, attentiveness, awareness, and presence.

---

7. Johnston, *Lord Teach Us to Pray*, 187.

Contemplative Prayer and the New Testament

> And when you come before God, don't turn that into a theatrical production either. All these people making a regular show out of their prayers, hoping for stardom! Do you think God sits in a box seat? Here's what I want you to do: Find a quiet, secluded place so you won't be tempted to role-play before God. Just be there as simply and honestly as you can manage. The focus will shift from you to God, and you will begin to sense God's grace.
>
> The world is full of so-called prayer warriors who are prayer-ignorant. They are full of formulas and programs and advice, peddling techniques for getting what you want from God. Don't fall for that nonsense. This is your Father you are dealing with. And he knows better than you what you need. With a God like this loving you, you can pray very simply. Like this . . . (Matt 6:5-7 MSG)

Across the centuries the great saints and mystics have written extensively on the mysteries to be discovered and experienced in the Lord's Prayer.

THE PRAYER JESUS TAUGHT

In Luke's Gospel the prayer Jesus gives is a response to the disciple's request:

> And it came about that while Jesus was praying in a certain place, after he had finished, one of His disciples said to Him, "Lord teach us to pray just as John taught his disciples to pray." (Luke 11:1)

Although Jesus provides the disciples—and us—with what has come to be known as "The Lord's Prayer," it is doubtful that the disciples were merely looking for a set prayer to recite. They were already familiar with many prayers such as the *Shema*. When I go to seek spiritual direction, what I want to know is not whether my spiritual director has some new beautiful-sounding prayer I can use, although she may very well share such prayers with me, but whether she has any insight as to how I might live more prayerfully, more consciously aware of divine presence and mystery. Indeed, as observed earlier, Bernard McGinn's extensive historical research has brought him to understand mysticism across the centuries, or at least one aspect of mysticism, as "an attempt to express a direct consciousness of God."[8] And so Jesus taught them to pray:

> Our Father in heaven,
> Reveal who you are.
> Set the world right;
> Do what's best—
> as above, so below.
> Keep us alive with three square meals.
> Keep us forgiven with you and forgiving others.
> Keep us safe from ourselves and the Devil.
> You're in charge!
> You can do anything you want!
> You're ablaze in beauty
> Yes. Yes. Yes.
>
> (Matt 6:9–13 MSG)

I suspect that what was behind the request the disciples made of Jesus, was a desire to have the sort of God consciousness, the sort of contemplative consciousness, Jesus had.

JESUS, THE CONTEMPLATIVE WISDOM OF GOD

Contemplation leads to enlightenment. For the prophets, enlightenment was most often described as *Ruach HaKodesh*, literally "Holy Spirit." Aryeh Kaplan explains:

> The level of enlightenment implied by *Ruach HaKodesh* involves a clarity of understanding, and enhancement of perception, an awareness of the spiritual, and often a complete change of personality.[9]

When Nicodemus is drawn to seek Jesus out, the first thing Nicodemus says is, "Rabbi, we know that you have come from God as a teacher; for no one can do these signs that You do unless God is

---

8. McGinn, *Foundations of Mysticism*, xvi.
9. Kaplan, *Bible and Meditation*, 17–18.

Contemplative Prayer and the New Testament

with him" (John 3:2 NASB). Notice that Nicodemus acknowledges both the wisdom of Jesus as a teacher, and the power of Jesus' actions. The prophets were profound in their revelation of divine truth, and channels through which spiritual force could flow. In the prophets, one sees the kind of presence, power, and wisdom that comes from deep meditation, from contemplative practice, which is precisely what we see in Jesus.

Modern Protestantism, as well as conservative Roman Catholicism, has frequently taken a rather magical or fantastic view of Jesus, so that Jesus is not really God with us, but only God pretending to be human. I am not attempting to suggest that Jesus was not divine, or that Jesus did not think of himself as divine, only that Jesus' knowledge of divinity was, as N. T. Wright says, knowing with a human mind and primarily as a sense of vocation—something that can only be known by living into it.[10] If Wright is, as I believe, correct, then meditation would have played a huge part in Jesus' self-knowledge. Jesus' wisdom and power, we can well believe, flowed from God through Jesus, but it was the contemplative life that made him an open channel for that wisdom, power, and presence. Compare these two texts, one from Ezekiel and one from Jesus of Nazareth:

> And as He spoke to me the Spirit entered me and set me on my feet; and I heard Him speaking to me I am sending you to them who are stubborn and obstinate children; and you shall say to them, "Thus says the Lord God." As for them whether they listen or not they will know that a prophet has been among them. (Ezek 2:2, 4, 5 NIV)

> If anyone is willing to do God's will, that person shall know of the teaching whether it is of God, or whether I speak of Myself. (John 7:17 NIV)

Kaplan states, "The ability to focus spiritual energy was a task that took great discipline and many years of intensive training... trying to obtain a clear message while in a mystical state."[11] Think of Jesus

---

10. Wright, *Jesus and the Victory*, 652–53.
11. Kaplan, *Bible and Meditation*, 27–31.

in the wilderness temptation or in the garden of Gethsemane. It is impossible for me to imagine that Jesus' insight into Scripture or life did not come from the discipline of meditative practice, that it was, so to speak, off the cuff.

JESUS AND SPIRITUAL AT-ONE-MENT

Many mystics tend to express their goal and ultimate desire as the longing for union, for communion, for atonement—for "at-one-ment" with God. T. S. Eliot caught it perfectly: "We must be still and still moving into another intensity for a further union, a deeper communion."[12] In *Will and Spirit*, Gerald May writes of union and belonging and love in this way:

> In spontaneously occurring unitive experiences one feels suddenly "swept up by life, caught in a suspended moment where time seems to stand still and awareness peaks in both of its dimensions, becoming at once both totally wide-awake and open. Everything in the immediate environment is experienced with awesome clarity, and the vast panorama of consciousness lies open. For the duration of the experience—which usually lasts not long—mental activity seems to be suspended. Preoccupations, misgivings, worries, and desires all seem to evaporate, leaving everything "perfect just as it is." Usually there are some reactive feelings that occur toward the end of the experience, feelings such as awe, wonder, expansiveness, freedom, warmth, love, and a sense of total truth or "rightness." After the experience is over, there is an almost invariable recollection of having been at one.[13]

Jesus is not only the embodiment of that contemplative stillness moving into "another intensity for a further union, a deeper communion," but he is, according to Saint Paul, the means of its full realization (Eph 1:9, 10).

---

12. Eliot, *Four Quartets*, 32.
13. May, *Will & Spirit*, 53–54.

Contemplative Prayer and the New Testament

THE SPIRITUALITY OF SAINT JOHN THE EVANGELIST

Similarly, it is obvious that both the fourth Gospel and the Book of Revelation—whether written by the same or different persons—were written by someone with a profoundly mystical consciousness, a state that one finds only among contemplatives. John of the Apocalypse and Ezekiel are comparable in the grandeur, mystery, and power of their visions. Their experience of divine glory is even much the same:

> As the appearance of the rainbow in the sky on a rainy day, so was the appearance of the surrounding radiance. Such was the appearance of the likeness of the glory of the Lord. And when I saw it, I fell on my face and heard a voice speaking. (Ezek 1:28)[14]
>
> His face was like the sun shining in its strength. And when I saw Him, I fell at his feet as a dead man. And he laid His right hand upon me saying, "Do not be afraid, I am the first and the last." (Rev 1:16 b, 17 REB)

Are we to think that the purity of heart necessary for receiving such visions, that the openness and receptivity of Ezekiel and John to these mystical cosmic experiences, had nothing to do with the disciplined practice of meditation? Such a notion is absurd to anyone at all acquainted with the spiritual and religious traditions of the world.

According to John's Gospel, on his last night, with time running out for saying the things that most needed saying, Jesus told his closest friends and disciples—who representatively include us—that he was in the Father and the Father was in him, making the Father, the Son, and the Holy Spirit, *one*. He told them that he was in them, and they were in him, and that the Holy Spirit would live in them always (John 14:9–17). Barry Ulanov translates Saint Augustine's quote of John like this: "He that believes in me goes

---

14. Kaplan, *Bible and Meditation*, 45.

into me; and he that goes into me has me."[15] And Jesus says if you want to know what eternal life is, if you want to know what real life is, it is this: "Eternal life is to know (to experience intimately) the only true God, and the Christ that God sent" (John 17:3). The breathtaking truth then is that in the mysticism of the fourth Gospel, in John's understanding of the teaching of Jesus, we are in God (the Father, the Son, and the Holy Spirit), and God (Father, Son and Holy Spirit) is in us. It all defies ordinary imagination, but here is a little story that may help.

JOHN 14 AND THE PARABLE OF THE SIEVE

A woman came to an old hermit living in a hut by the sea. "Teach me," she asked the hermit who was known for his great wisdom, "what it means to be at once both fully in the presence of God, and for my soul to be full of the Spirit of Christ." He picked up a sieve and said, "First, we, must walk down to the sea." When they reached the rocky shore with the tide coming in, the hermit handed her the sieve and said, "Now show me how to collect water in this sieve." She scooped water into the sieve again and again, but it only poured out each time. Finally, she handed the sieve back to the hermit saying, "I don't know how, perhaps you might show me if there is a way." The old man gently took the sieve and flung it out as far he was able into the sea. It floated there briefly, and then sank. "There," he said, "the sieve is now both completely in the ocean's water and it is full of water." This is the spiritual life—the contemplative life.

THE MYSTICISM OF PAUL THE APOSTLE

Saint Paul, who is credited with writing thirteen of the twenty-seven books of the New Testament, is frequently read by scholars, clergy, and laity, as if Paul could be summed up as an academic writing learned treatises on theology. But Paul was one of the

---

15. Ulanov, *Prayers of Saint Augustine*, 13.

Contemplative Prayer and the New Testament

greatest mystics to ever live and must be read as such. Albert Schweitzer's *The Mysticism of Paul the Apostle*,[16] first published in 1931, remains an important piece of literature in Pauline studies. It is generally agreed that when Paul writes of a man who experienced ineffable visions and revelations in 2 Corinthians 12:1–4, he is talking about himself:

> It may do no good, but I must go on with my boasting; I come now to visions and revelations granted by the Lord. I know a man who fourteen years ago (whether in the body or out of the body, I do not know—God knows) was caught up as far as the third heaven. And I know that this same man (whether in the body or apart from the body, I do not know—God knows) was caught up into paradise, and heard words so secret that human lips may not repeat them. (2 Cor 12:1–4 REB)

In *The Spirit of the Disciplines*, Dallas Willard asserts, "It is in the light of Paul's *practice*, the way he lived, that we must interpret the statements about his experience and behavior and what *we* are to do (italics his)."[17] We know that for Paul, religious asceticism, exercise, and disciplined training were essential to the spiritual life. To the Corinthians, Paul writes:

> You know (do you not?) that at the sports all the runners run the race, though only one wins the prize. Like them, run to win! But every athlete goes into strict training. They do it to win a fading wreath; we, a wreath that never fades. (1 Cor 9:24–25 NEB)

And to Timothy (whether Paul himself wrote the Pastoral Epistles is irrelevant to our discussion here) Paul says:

> Keep yourself in training for the practice of religion. The training of the body does bring limited benefit, but the limits of religion are without limit, since it holds promise not only for this life but for the life to come. (1 Tim 4:7–9 NEB)

---

16. Schweitzer, *Mysticism of Paul the Apostle*.
17. Willard, *Spirit of the Disciplines*, 105.

"In short," says William Johnston, "the theology of Paul is based not only on a historical event in the past but also on a living mystical experience. This is what I mean when I say that mystical experience is the core of authentic theology."[18]

I have been looking for an apppropriate place—and this seems as good a location as any—to briefly note that the expression "in Christ" or some cognate of it, occurs 164 times in the writings of Saint Paul. In speaking of the Christian life as being "in Christ," Paul is describing the Christian Way as living in vital and intimate union with Christ. And when he writes of being "in the Spirit," or of the "Spirit in us," he speaks of "our living, moving, and having our being in a *pneuma* element which is the very breath of life."[19] The Scottish Protestant scholar James Stewart observed:

> If one seeks for the most characteristic sentences the Apostle Paul ever wrote, they will be found not where he is refuting legalists, or vindicating his apostleship, or meditating on eschatological hope, or giving practical ethical guidance to the Church, but where his intense intimacy with Christ comes to expression. Everything that religion meant for Paul is focused for us in such great words as these: "I live, yet not I, but Christ liveth in me" (Gal. 2:20).[20]

Stewart went on to note that Paul was not writng systematic theolgy, nor is Paul's work to be understood as a treatise on *justification*—the center of Pauline theology is a personal and intimate union of life with Christ, through Christ, and in Christ.

Paul's spiritual practice was the practice of the presence of Christ. His own personal practice included the spiritual disciplines of silence and solitude—both of which are indicative of some deep method of meditation. So for instance, immediately after his Damascus Road experience and his baptism into Christ by Ananias in the City of Damascus, Paul flees the comforts of home and position and disappears into the solitude of the wild Arabian

---

18. Johnston, *Lord Teach Us to Pray*, 192.
19. Stewart, *Man in Christ*, 157.
20. Ibid., 147.

desert where for fourteen years he does not "consult with flesh and blood" (Acts: 9:9,11).

PAUL'S KENOSIS HYMN—PHILIPPIANS 2:5-11

What is thought to have originally been a Christian hymn (Phil 2:5-11) is one of the most signifcant passages in the New Testament on the nature of Christian spirituality. There is not sufficient space here to do an exegesis of that entire pericope, but notice the following verses:

> Let the same mind be in you that was in Christ Jesus,
> who, though he was in the form of God,
> did not regard equality with God
> as something to be exploited,
> but emptied himself,
> taking the form of a slave,
> being born in human likeness.
>
> (Phil 2:5-7a NRSV)

Christian spirituality is the way of self-emptying, the Greek word here is *kenosis*, for it is the Way of Christ.

You may remember the story of the young man who rode his horse furiously over a great distance seeking spiritual guidance in acquiring wisdom. The teacher, doubting his readiness, invited him to sit down and enjoy a quiet cup of tea. Impatiently the young man sat down while the teacher began pouring tea into his cup. The tea filled the cup, spilled onto the table, across the table, and onto the floor, but the teacher kept pouring. Finally the young man jumped up. "Stop it!" he shouted. "Can't you see the cup is full? It can't hold any more." The teacher quit pouring and looked quietly and sadly at the young man. "Yes," he said, "it is too full. And how can you expect to receive anything unless you present yourself as an empty cup?" The aim of Christian contemplation is not to have a blank mind, if that were even possible, but to empty the heart and mind so as to be able to be filled with Christ. The aim of self-emptying Christian meditation is to present an empty cup.

The Christian poet and mystic T. S. Eliot, in "East Coker," found in his *Four Quartets*, furnishes perhaps some of the best commentary on Philippians 2:5–7:

> I said to my soul, be still and wait without hope
> For hope would be hope for the wrong thing; wait without
> love
> For love would be love of the wrong thing; there is yet faith
> But the faith and the love and the hope are all in the waiting.
> Wait without thought, for you are not yet ready for thought:
> So the darkness will be the light, and the stillness the dancing.[21]

> Shall I say it again? In order to arrive there,
> To arrive where you are, to get from where you are not,
> You must go by a way wherein there is no ecstasy.
> In order to arrive at what you do not know
> You must go by a way which is the way of ignorance.
> in order to possess what you do not possess
> you must go by the way of dispossession.
> In order to arrive at what you are not
> you must go through the way in which you are not.[22]

Henri Nouwen was right: the way of contemplative spirituality is the way of downward mobility. Saint Francis was right: mystic practice is the the pursuit of "Lady Poverty"—of dispossession. Saint Paul was right: to be filled one must become empty—empty of concepts, images, intellecutual theories, surging emotions and swirling thoughts, obsessions, compulsions, addictions, fabricated self-images, empty of all little faiths, hopes, loves, desires, and loyalties until nothing but Christ alone remains.

---

21. Eliot, *Four Quartets*, 28.
22. Ibid., 29.

Contemplative Prayer and the New Testament

FROM THE HOUSE OF DEUTERONOMY TO THE TEMPLE OF THE APOCALYPSE

But we said at the outset that there is a contemplative theme in Scripture running all the way from Genesis through Revelation. So in addition to what was noted earlier regarding John and the Apocalypse, notice Revelation 22:2 and 14, which returns to the "tree" imagery of Genesis, and notice Revelation 21:22, where John describes the New Jerusalem, the heavenly city, beyond space, and time, and death like this: "And I saw no temple in it, for the Lord God, the Almighty, and the Lamb, are its temple." Holding that in mind, read Psalm 27:4–5.

> One thing I have asked from the Lord, that I shall seek:
> That I may dwell in the house of the Lord all the days of my life,
> To behold the beauty of the Lord
> And to meditate in His temple.
>
> (Ps 27:4–5 NASB)

The spiritual life then according to both the Old and New Testaments, is a life lived in God and Christ the Lamb. It is a life in which our whole being is said to be devoted to praying in the "temple." But the temple in which we pray is not the temple of stone; rather it is the Living God and Christ the Lamb. In this placeless place, in this state, says the poet, "I behold the beauty of the Lord." In the Torah, there is a seldom-noticed verse with large implications for understanding Judeo-Christian spirituality as a spirituality of presence, and as inherently mystical and contemplative. It is a verse which ought to be read in connection with Revelation 21:22. I am thinking of Deuteronomy 33:27. With both complete simplicity and amazing profundity, it says: "The eternal God is a dwelling place" (Deut 33:27a). God is the contemplative's temple.

From the Stone Age to Thomas Merton

THE BIBLICAL CONTINUITY OF CONTEMPLATIVE PRACTICE

In the Hebrew Scriptures, we find a spirituality, a religion, a faith and wisdom of spiritual presence as the contemplative experience of divine mystery. This melody continues to play beyond Malachi—and beyond the Second Temple era. In the New Testament, from the Gospel according to Matthew through Revelation, we find a people (Jesus, the apostles, disciples, great saints, and ordinary believers) who knew prayer as words, as intimate conversation with God, but also as something deeper than thought and higher than human discourse—contemplation in its truest sense.

FOUR

Contemplative Prayer and Monasticism

Many are avidly seeking but they alone find who remain in continual silence.... Those who delight in a multitude of words, even though they say admirable things, are empty within. If you love truth, be a lover of silence. Silence like the sunlight will illuminate you in God and will deliver you from the phantoms of ignorance. Silence will unite you to God.

ISAAC OF NINEVEH[1]

Surrender consists, not in doing great heroic deeds about which the self can brag, but simply in accepting whatever God sends, and not seeking to change it (unless it is God's will for it to be changed). Full surrender is full peace. If we are restless and concerned about things formerly renounced, we have not genuinely surrendered. Surrender is the source of true peace. If we aren't at peace, it is because our surrender is not complete.

FENELON IN *SPIRITUAL LETTERS*[2]

---

1. Merton, *Contemplative Prayer*, 39.
2. Fenelon, *Let Go*, 34.

EASTERN MONASTICISIM: THE QUESTION

AT ITS HEART, EASTERN monastic spirituality represented the human longing for self-surrender. The Mennonites, as heirs to the radical Reformation, have a German word that expresses it perfectly—*gelassenheit*. It is probably impossible to really translate this word, but it means something like: "An acceptance, or yielding, or self-surrender and the peace that goes with it." Desert monasticism was essentially a flight from the world, a renunciation of the greed, materialism, and violence of the world in which even the church was becoming saturated. As has often been pointed out, it was a flight from an increasingly worldly and superficial Christian church—they were fleeing "the world in the church."

We are all, even in our spirituality, influenced by our social and cultural context. You may have heard the saying: "Christianity went to Greece and it became a philosophy. Then it went to Rome and became an institution. And finally, it went to America where it became an enterprise." People in the Eastern Mediterranean world at that time saw the question of how the soul might transcend the body and all materialism as crucial to the spiritual life. Any reasonably informed person in that third and fourth-century world would have been well acquainted with the mix of Platonism, Stoicism, Gnosticism, Manichaeism, and Neoplatonism that was so integral to the eastern Mediterranean. How, they wanted to know, can the body be brought under control and overcome so that the soul may transcend its limitations and the evil that surrounds us? The exploration of that question sometimes led them to practices we might consider a little bizarre, and for some of them ideas that were somewhat suspect. Be that as it may, these Christian men and women of the desert sought virtue through the analysis and avoidance of evil in order that they might become insensitive to the values and ways of the world. As George Lane wrote:

> Once perfect control over the body and material things is achieved, one can move to the contemplative stage where another kind of asceticism takes place, that of the mind. The mind is systematically purged of all images, symbols,

and concepts... Hence the object of the contemplative life is to gradually empty the mind in order for God to come in and fill it. And this, they thought, is the very perfection of all Christian and human life.[3]

CHRISTIAN KENOSIS

One of the most significant Christian responses to the prevailing Greek philosophical schools of the time came from the early church father Origen (185–225 CE). Origen proposed a theology of Christocentric asceticism and mysticism. Human perfection for Origen, although himself a great scholar, was not to be found in knowledge but in love and the works of charity. Renunciation, asceticism, and contemplation were not for Origen the end of the spiritual life, but means of conquering evil inclinations and achieving the perfect love of Christ, who is the actual end and aim of spirituality. Robert Jonas, in his essay "Christian Prayer: Silence & Dancing Between Knowing and Unknowing," writes this in regard to contemplation as it came to be practiced by the desert monks:

> In the first centuries after Jesus' life and death, most Desert/monks/writers were familiar with silence—their own silence, and the silence of God. Quite often they emphasized "purity of heart" and a letting go of all thoughts that were not directed to God. They suggested that to enter into the light (or the darkness) of God's presence one should first focus the mind with a simple prayer. Single lines or phrases from the Psalms were often used for this purpose: "Oh God, come to my assistance, Make haste to help me," or "Son of the Living God have mercy on me." Sometimes the one praying is counseled to recite this short prayer in rhythm with each breath. St. Athanasius suggested that one simply "breath Christ." Sometimes, these mystical theologians understood the letting go of one's thoughts and emotions as the "emptying" (Greek: *kenosis*) that is mentioned by St. Paul in Philippians 2:4ff, where Christ "emptied himself." In silence, these mystical

3. Lane, *Christian Spirituality*, 15.

theologians sensed a unity with God that cannot be experienced if one is caught up in one's own thinking *about* God. Their spiritual practice is sometimes called the *via negative* or the way of unknowing—versus the *via affirmative*, which proceeds by the way of what we *can* know about God through our senses.[4]

THE JESUS PRAYER

Beginning in the fourth century, it is possible to see the development of those elements that would come to constitute a contemplative method of praying known as the "Jesus Prayer." The basic form of this prayer is a short sentence, designed for frequent repetition, which is addressed to Jesus. Modeled after the Publican's prayer in Luke 8:9–14 it is usually phrased as: "Lord Jesus Christ, Son of God, have mercy on me." The four distinguishable elements of this prayer are:

1) Devotion to the Holy Name "Jesus," which is felt to act in a semi-sacramental way as a source of power and grace.

2) The appeal for divine mercy, accompanied by a keen sense of compunction and inward grief (*penthos*).

3) The discipline of frequent repetition.

4) The quest for inner silence or stillness (*hesuchia*), that is to say, for imageless, nondiscursive prayer.[5]

Kallistos Ware says in *The Study of Spirituality* that there is evidence for the last three of these elements in monastic Egypt—if not among the Coptic monks then at least in the writings of Evagrius.[6] Simon Tugwell also, writing in *The Study of Spirituality*, notes that for Evagrius: "Prayer is the highest and most proper activity of the mind, but, paradoxically it means, at its purest, the putting away

---

4. Jonas, "Christian Prayer," 3–4. Also: Woods, *Christian Spirituality*, 134–35.

5. Jones et al, *Study of Spirituality*, 176.

6. Ibid., 177.

Contemplative Prayer and Monasticism

of thoughts. . . . all that is left is the formless mind as an intense yearning for God."[7]

The standard form of the Jesus Prayer is first found in *The Life of Philemon*, an Egyptian monk of probably the sixth century. In time it became virtually synonymous with *Hesychasm*. The term *Hesychasm*, from Greek *hesuchia*, means "quiet" or "stillness." In its general sense, it simply means the adoption and use of the Jesus Prayer. But more narrowly Hesychastic spirituality refers to someone who practices interiority—seeks God in the silence of the heart. There are three basic features associated with the Jesus Prayer or Hesychasm:

1) The aspirant sits on a low stool with head resting on beard or chest so that the gaze is fixed on the heart.

2) Breathing is slow and rhythmic to promote calmness and concentration. Breathing should be in tempo and coordinated with the prayer. The first part of the prayer, "Lord Jesus Christ, Son of God" is said while breathing in. The rest of the prayer is said while breathing out.

3) As the breathing becomes slow and rhythmic and calm, the monk searches inwardly for the place of the heart by imagining the breath entering through the nostrils and passing down into the lungs until it reaches the heart. In this way the intellect descends into the heart so that heart and mind become one.

4) Having found the place of the heart one begins the recitation of the Jesus Prayer. "From this point on as soon as a thought arises it is expelled by the invocation of Jesus Christ."[8]

In our rather casual investigation, it should be obvious that contemplative prayer is somewhat paradoxical in that it shows signs of both continuity and discontinuity; that is, contemplative prayer is not static but rather, while remaining connected to past

---

7. Ibid., 172.
8. Ibid., 180–81, 242–46.

forms, is adapted by its practitioners to the needs and circumstances of the age in which they live.

MONKS AND MYSTICS OF THE ORDINARY LIFE

With this in mind, I wonder what it might mean for the church, for the world, for families, and for each Christian man and woman, if we saw ourselves in our ordinary lives as Christian monks dedicated to contemplative living—awakened spirits who understand that their practice of prayer and meditation is their part in God's vast work of transformation and the triumph of love.

CONTEMPLATIVE PRAYER AND THE WESTERN MEDEVIAL MONASTICS

Saint Benedict, though others actually established religious communities before him, is usually acknowledged as the founder of Western Monasticism. He was well acquainted with the disorderly side of monastic life. In his first experience, at a place called Vicovaro, the other monks who had gathered around Benedict in community tried to poison him—perhaps because of his attempts to get them to lead a more fervent life. Eventually, after leaving Vicovaro, Benedict founded twelve different monasteries on Mt. Subiaco. Around 528 CE he founded the Monte Cassino monastery, where during the last years of his life he wrote the famous Benedictine Rule. Norvene Vest has written a wonderful commentary/meditation on the Benedictine Rule which you may want to read. As the guide for the spiritual life of the Benedictine community, this rule has continued to influence all monastic life in the West for fifteen hundred years.[9]

---

9. Vest, *Preferring Christ*.

SPIRITUALITY OF THE COMMUNITY

Daily life in the monastery was carried out with a simple rhythm of liturgical prayer, manual labor, and *lectio divina*, or "sacred reading." Liturgical prayer was chiefly the chanting of the divine office in choir according to the set canonical hours. Daily manual labor, preferably farm work in the beginning but later study as well, helped the monks avoid idleness and provide for the needs of the community. Work was, and is, seen in the Benedictine tradition as a kind of prayer itself. *Lection divina*, or the quiet reading of Scripture, was considered meditation, and in turn could become contemplation as the words, thoughts, and images dropped away. However, Benedict did not use the word "contemplation" in his rule. For Benedict, perfection was not so much experienced in tranquility and contemplation like the angelic life sought by the Eastern monks, but rather in charity, humility, and obedience lived out in community. It is interesting to note that the Latin word for "obedience"—*audio*—means "to listen." Contemplative prayer as conceived among the medieval monastics was, then, primarily that of *lectio divina*—metaphorically a dance composed of four steps:

1) *Lectio* (sacred or prayerful reading) involves reading, or reciting, a passage of Scripture slowly, quietly, gently.

2) *Meditatio* (reflection) is when a word or a phrase from the passage is repeated slowly so that its meaning begins to sink deep into the soul.

3) *Oratio* is the expressing of one's spontaneous emotional or prayerful response to God's loving presence as experienced in the reading.

4) *Contemplatio*, in which discursive thoughts evaporate and concepts simply drop away as one rests in God's mysterious presence without words or images.

There was, of course, not just one but multiple methods of meditation and prayer developed by laypeople and monks, and in convents and monasteries.

DOMINICAN SPIRITUALITY

The Order of Preachers, founded by Dominic de Guzman eight hundred years ago, has had among its sustaining mottos and guiding principles "*Contemplare et contemplate aliis*" ("To contemplate and to share with others the fruits of one's contemplation"). Saint Dominic's method, or methods, of meditation or contemplative prayer was typical of a thirteenth-century monk:[10]

> Bowing by profoundly inclining his head before the altar he would slowly chant: "Glory be to the Father, and to the Son and to the Holy Spirit."
>
> Outstretched on the ground he would recite Luke 18:13 (A prayer used by the Desert Fathers and Mothers), "O God, be merciful to me a sinner."
>
> Deep in prayer, he appeared to be meditating upon the words of God, and he seemed to repeat them to himself in a sweet voice.
>
> He appeared then to be listening carefully as if to hear something spoken from the altar. If one had seen his great devotion as he stood erect and prayed, he would certainly have thought that he was observing a prophet, first speaking with an angel or with God himself, then listening, then silently thinking of those things which had been revealed to him.
>
> After the canonical hours he quickly withdrew to some solitary place. To his cell or elsewhere, and recollected himself in the presence of God. He would sit quietly. And after the sign of the cross, begin to read from a book opened before him.
>
> The holy custom of our father seems, as it were, to resemble the prophetic mountain of the Lord in as much as he quickly passed upwards from reading to prayer, from prayer to meditation, and from meditation to contemplation.

---

10. "The Nine Ways of Prayer of St. Dominic" was written by an anonymous author, probably at Bologna, between 1260 and 1288.

Contemplative Prayer and Monasticism

Saint Dominic seems to have engaged in a number of meditative practices—chanting, music, gazing at the crucifix, reciting Scripture sentences, and *lectio divina*—which carried him into a deeper consciousness of God, into a contemplative state, into wisdom, and sustained him in his apostolic ministry.

SAINT FRANCIS—ARDENT LOVER OF LADY POVERTY

The story of Saint Francis of Assisi (1182–1226) is well known. He was the overly indulged child of a wealthy family. His father was a cloth merchant and land owner. As a young man, he showed little interest in either his studies or the family business. More than anything else, Francis wanted to enjoy himself. People liked him and he liked drinking, dancing, and partying. Not unusual for someone his age, he daydreamed of becoming a knight and winning fame in battle.

When Francis was twenty, war broke out between the citizens of Assisi and Perugia. With his expensive armor, horse, and mantle he joined the army. When he and the other knights and soldiers of Assisi came under attack by a vastly superior Perugian force, they fled, and were slaughtered as they did so. The battlefield was covered with the dead and wounded, the mutilated screaming in agony. Most of the survivors were put to death, but Francis, dressed as a wealthy aristocrat, was taken prisoner and held for ransom. He suffered for nearly a year in a dark, wet, disease-ridden dungeon while he waited for his father to pay the ransom. During this time, Francis became dangerously ill. Even after he had made it back home, his recovery was long and slow. It was during his time in prison that Francis began to experience visions. Francis, of course, did not speak of experiencing visions, but rather of receiving visions as gifts from God.

Oddly, once home and recovered, Francis didn't seem all that changed. He still partied with as much abandon as ever, and still wanted the fame of a knight. When a call for knights for the Fourth Crusade came, he saw again a chance to realize his dream.

He actually boasted that he would return to Assisi a prince, but Francis never got any farther than a day's ride from Assisi. He had a dream in which God told him, "Serve the master and not the slave." It was utterly humiliating. He was laughed at and ridiculed as a coward.

One day sometime after this, Francis was riding his horse though the countryside when he encountered a leper. Instead of keeping his distance as required, Francis dismounted and embraced the leper. As he rode away he felt an incredible sense of freedom, a certain ecstasy.

Francis now began turning more and more to God. He spent many hours at a remote mountain hideaway as well as in old and quiet churches around Assisi praying, seeking, nursing lepers. People would see him in the streets looking happy but distracted. They thought he looked as if he was in love and asked him if that was so. He would reply that yes, he was in love with the most beautiful woman in the world, by which he meant his passion for the spiritual quality he called Lady Poverty.

On another occasion, while praying before a Byzantine crucifix in the church of San Damiano, he heard the voice of Christ say, "Rebuild my church, for it has fallen into ruin." At first, he thought this meant to literally rebuild this dilapidated church which had fallen into disrepair, and so he begged bricks and repaired churches all around Assisi with his own hands. Only later did he understand his vision metaphorically and spiritually. He began preaching around Assisi and was soon joined by the eight loyal followers who constituted the beginning of the Franciscan Order.

Because Saint Francis wrote so little himself, particularly in regard to Christian spirituality, Bernard McGinn is somewhat dismissive of him as a mystic. I find this a little puzzling. It seems to me that Saint Francis, to a very large degree, epitomizes the contemplative ideal of allowing one's very life to become prayer. But there are other marks as well. Giving away his armor seems to represent mystical self-surrender, his embracing of the leper the humility and compassion of the mystic, while his dreams and visions speak of mystical insight. And when the Christ figure speaks

Contemplative Prayer and Monasticism

to him from the Byzantine cross, it is not difficult or unreasonable to think that he is practicing meditation in the sense of icon gazing. His visions, beginning in prison, may very well have to do in some way with his devastating illness, but can we not imagine that this intelligent, lonely, and ill young prisoner prayed prayers of deep intensity? I am thinking, obviously, of the sort of transformative experience of which Alexander Solzhenitsyn spoke when he wrote that it was while lying on a rancid bed of straw in the cold of a Siberian prison camp that he comprehended the nature of good and evil and began to be able to say: "Thank you prison. Thank you for having been there in my life."[11] What we see in Francis's spiritual transformation are pivotal events that can only be described as contemplative.

However, the mysticism of Saint Francis becomes especially vivid in his devotion to poverty as a spiritual discipline. For Francis, the pursuit of poverty becomes a contemplative practice and therefore the way to God. In the Franciscan allegory of the *Sacred Commerce of St. Francis and Lady Poverty*, probably written about ten years after his death, Francis is portrayed as the suitor of Lady Poverty, the personification of perfect love and knowledge of God. Here, "Holy poverty," is said to be ". . . the foundation and guardian of all virtues," and, the kingdom of heaven as belonging "to those who, of their own will, a spiritual intention, and a desire for eternal goods, possess nothing of this earth."[12] Contemplative prayer reveals what Johannes Metz in *Poverty of Spirit* referred to as "the precipitous depths of our poverty." Practicing the spiritual poverty of the Beatitudes, said Metz, brings mystical awareness and insight into the true nature of the human condition: "We are so poor," says Metz, "that even our poverty is not our own; it belongs to the mystery of God."[13] For Francis, embracing poverty was the practice of self-surrender and the realization of the presence of God.

---

11. Solzhenitsyn, *Gulag Archipelago*, 2:616–17.
12. Armstrong et al, *Francis of Assisi—The Saint*, 529.
13. Metz, *Poverty of Spirit*, 52.

Some have thought Francis among the greatest of saints and icons of the cruciform life. Others have thought him crazy, a fool or madman. But O, to be mad like Francis of Assisi.

FROM SAINT DOMINIC TO THE LATE MIDDLE AGES

From Saint Dominic to the late Middle Ages, the Christian church produced some of the greatest mystics ever known—pure contemplatives. It also produced, in the Protestant Reformation, the negation of the contemplative life. Sometime near the end of the thirteenth century, two books written in Middle English by an anonymous monk—whom many believe was himself a Dominican—appeared: *The Cloud of Unknowing* and the *Book of Privy Counseling*. *The Cloud* insists that one can think and think and think about God all he or she wants, but eventually will come to that with which the intellect cannot deal. God must, therefore, be sought through intense contemplation, motivated by love, and stripped of all thought. In this way one touches the reality of God and enters into communion with God.

> For God can well be loved, but cannot be thought. By love God can be grasped and held, but by thought neither grasped nor held. And therefore, though it may be good at times to think specifically of the kindness and excellence of God, and though this may be a light and a part of contemplation, all the same, in the work of contemplation itself, it must be cast down and covered with a cloud of forgetting. And you must step above it stoutly but deftly, with a devout and delightful stirring of love, and struggle to pierce that darkness above you; and beat on that thick cloud of unknowing with a sharp dart of longing love, and do not give up, whatever happens.[14]
>
> —from *The Cloud of Unknowing*

---

14. Anonymous, *Cloud of Unknowing* and *Book of Privy Counseling*, 54–55. Also see: Johnston, *Mysticism of the Cloud of Unknowing*.

Contemplative Prayer and Monasticism

The method of letting go of all thoughts, concepts, ideas, words and images is through the repetition of a single simple word. The author of the *Cloud of Unknowing* thought that the one word should be "God." In this way, one would, the monk believed, come to rest in a blind, naked feeling of being—of "being in Love."

FINDING GOD IN ALL THINGS

The Jesuits, as an Order, do not fit, at least technically, into the history of the contemplative tradition. However, the Jesuits have been and are such a powerful force both in the church and the larger world that it is imposible not to say something about Ignatian spirituality. Ignatius of Loyola, the fourteenth-century founder of the Jesuits, believed that God speaks to us not only through thoughts and memories, but also through our imagination. In Jesuit spirituality, praying with thoughts and with the imagination is considered to be contemplation and is, therefore, quite different from the sort of prayer we have been exploring here—prayer which lets go of thoughts and images. Many have found the Ignatian Spiritual Exercises, which employ imagination, to be hugely helpful, especially in matters of discernment. And one will find a considerable number of Jesuit monks, priests, and teachers who are among the profoundest practitioners of both contemplation as a quieting of the heart and mind and praying discursively. Certainly the Jesuit motto, "Finding God in all things," expresses the deep intent of both ways, of both *kataphatic* and *apophatic* spirituality and mysticism.

SIXTEENTH-CENTURY ENVIRONMENT OF ST. TERESA AND JOHN OF THE CROSS

The sixteenth century was a time of dramatic changes both within and outside of Spain. Geographic explorations and discoveries were both intense and numerous. The Lutheran Reformation had been consolidated outside of Spain, and with it the rise of independent Scripture studies and the use of extemporaneous prayer. The Renaissance thought of Erasmus, what became known in Spain as Erasmianism, spoke to the longing of many Christians for prayer as an experience of intimacy and spirituality in place of traditional religiosity. This is the environmental context in which Teresa of Avila and Saint John of the Cross must be understood.

Teresa of Avila wrote of a prayer of quiet that becomes a passive experience of prayer leading ultimately to union with God, prayer as a state in which the soul experiences an extraordinary peace and rest, accompanied by delight or pleasure in contemplating God as present. Such prayer requires the stilling of the faculties of memory and will and intellect so as to be occupied with the one necessary thing. This is contemplation as a detachment from all but God's loving will.

For Saint John of the Cross, contemplation is beyond the normal thought processes. It is imageless and wordless. It is mystery. For the Sanjuanist, the end of contemplation is that mystical grace which is the loving inflow of God. Contemplation is divine wisdom; it is loving, tranquil, peaceful, and comes without our knowing from where or how it comes. Saint John did not write anything like a manual on the how of contemplation; instead, much of his thought is expressed in the beautiful Spanish poetry he composed:

> What a peaceful life
> the one that flees worldly noise
> and follows the secret
> path, by which have gone
> the few wise ones that have come into the world;
> their heart does not become confused
> "Song of the Solitary Life"[15]
>
> The peaceful night
> paired with the rising dawn,
> the silent music,

---

15. For parallel Spanish English See Zorrilla, *Saint John of the Cross*, 42. For more on the mystic poetry of Saint John of the Cross, see McGinn, *Essential Writings of Christian Mysticism*, 460–64; Woods, *Christian Spirituality*; Jones et al, *Study of Spirituality*, 364–76.

the echoing solitude,
the supper that delights and wins the heart.
Spiritual Canticle I[16]

However, my aim here is not to explore the details of the methods employed by Saint John of the Cross, or all the nuances of his spiritual theology, but to identify the constant link of contemplation in Christian thought and practice across the centuries.

PROTESTANTISM AND CONSERVATIVE ROMAN CATHOLICISM

This is perhaps the best place to suggest that one reason many Christians in Protestant churches have no sense of this historical continuity is that they feel no real connection with the Christians who lived between the time of the martyrs and Martin Luther, what some Protestant historians have called, "The thousand years without a bath."[17] The Protestant Reformation, a true child of the Enlightenment, emphasized a spirituality that was entirely *kataphatic*; that is, that God is to be found through our senses and our minds. With the one exception of the Quakers, every Protestant denomination focuses on spiritual practice as reading Scripture studiously, listening to sermons, and praying with words either out loud or in one's own mind. In fact, many Protestants are quite suspicious of words like "spirituality," and fear that if they become still, open, and receptive, they might be overcome by demonic forces.

This, obviously, does not explain the fear many fundamentalist Roman Catholics have of contemplative prayer. I was born and grew up in California's Central Valley. When my older brother was still alive, and just the two of us left, I would often visit him in Bakersfield. While driving I would sometimes turn on the radio to relieve the monotony. What I discovered is that there were only four types of radio programs available: conservative talk radio,

---

16. Ibid., 62.
17. Delahoyde, "Medieval Period," para. 2.

Protestant fundamentalist radio, country music radio, and conservative Roman Catholic radio. Whenever I listened for a little while to this last "genre," I would usually hear contemplative prayer attacked as satanic. How anyone can think that sitting quietly in the loving presence of God, with no other intent than to be with God, to welcome God ever deeper into one's soul, is evil, is simply beyond me.

Thomas Merton in his *A Course in Christian Mysticism*, suggested to the young monks he was teaching at the Abbey of Gethsmani that the ruthlessness with which the Inquisition sought to stamp out most mysticism as heretical had to do with issues of fear and control. He said:

> It will be seen that the chief concern of the Inquisition was not with the Bible or mysticism as such but as preached to the laity. In so many words, too deep an interest in the interior life was considered dangerous for all but the experts. Lay people were to be confined to "safe" exterior practices of devotion.[18]

The problem for the religious establishment can be framed like this: What is the institution and its official representatives to do if ordinary laypeople practice contemplation and experience a depth of life, of Christian faith, and of wisdom that the bishops, priests, and pastors know nothing about?

SUMMARY AND TRANSITION

But I digress. Robert Jonas furnishes a good historical summary up through the Middles Ages and a transition to the modern era:

> Over the centuries, monasteries and convents evolved their own favorite methods of prayer and meditation, drawing from Scripture, tradition and experience. Some emphasized silent meditation or contemplation, while others emphasized sacred liturgies and the Eucharist, a prayerful reading of Scripture, repetitive prayer, or

---

18. Merton, *Course in Christian Mysticism*, 164.

prayers of intercession, gratitude and praise. Some religious orders preferred to walk the *via negativa* and the *via affirmativa* simultaneously in their daily offices by including extended periods of silence in their rich liturgical experiences.[19]

What has been discovered over and over again is that the deeper our practice of any of the classical forms of prayer and meditation, the more spiritually awake and aware we become, and the more there is a shift from self-consciousness to God-consciousness.

---

19. Jonas, "Christian Prayer," para. 8.

FIVE

Contemplative Prayer and Contemporary Christianity

> Intellect by itself only gets us so far. It has a share in gratefulness, but only a share. Our intellect should be alert enough to look through the predictable husks of things to their core and find there a kernel of surprise. That in itself is a demanding task. But truthfulness also demands that the intellect be sufficiently humble, that is, sufficiently down to earth to know its limits. The gift character of everything can be recognized, but it cannot be proved—not by the intellect alone, at any rate. Proof lies in living. And there is more to living than the intellect can grasp.
>
> BROTHER DAVID STEINDL-RAST[1]

THOMAS MERTON

THOMAS MERTON (1915–1968) WAS perhaps the most influential Roman Catholic of twentieth-century North America. His

---

1. Steindl-Rast, *Gratefulness*, 13.

Contemplative Prayer and Contemporary Christianity

autobiography, *The Seven Story Mountain*, was a bestseller and responsible for the conversion of a large number of modern men and women to Christianity. Perhaps even more significant is the renewal of faith and deepening of spiritual life experienced by many, many more. He wrote over sixty books, and numerous poems and articles on monastic spirituality, social justice, nonviolence, and the nuclear arms race.

Merton entered the Abbey of Gethsemane in 1941, a community of monks of the Order of Cistercians of the Strict Observance (Trappist), the most ascetic of Roman Catholic monastic orders. Merton remained a Trappist monk until the time of his death. During his last years, he became deeply interested in Asian religions, particularly Zen Buddhism, and in promoting East-West dialogue. It was during a trip to a conference on East-West monastic dialogue that Merton died in Bangkok on December 10, 1968, the victim of an accidental electrocution. The date marked the twenty-seventh anniversary of his entrance into Gethsemani.

Some have found Merton's belief that contemplative practice furnishes common ground for dialogue between Christianity and Buddhism to be a little disquieting. However, the essential fact remains that Merton lived and died as a Trappist monk in the Catholic Church. What he said in defense of Teilhard de Chardin—a paleontologist, mystic, Jesuit, and priest—could just as easily be applied to Merton himself: "I do not think any responsible theologian who takes the trouble to interpret the author's true meaning will find in it anything he can condemn." He went on to write in this same essay:

> The risks that Teihard de Chardin demands of us are therefore, in no way the perils of modernism, of naturalism, of scientism. On the contrary, this scientist is speaking above all as a mystic. That is to say, he speaks the language of Patristic wisdom, which is basically contemplative and mystical rather than technical and exact. He is a scientist who writes as a poet, and writes for prospective saints, rather than for his fellow scientists as such. He is above all a priest, a minister of Christ, one sent by Christ, with a mission to "love the world" as Christ loved

it, and therefore to seek and find in it all the good which is hidden there and which Christ died on the cross to recover. Only in these priestly and Eucharist perspectives can we really understand the great work of Teilhard de Chardin...[2]

Or we might say it is as a Catholic monk and Christian mystic and contemplative that Thomas Merton himself must finally be understood. Jon Sweeney offers a clarifying and helpful perspective:

> Some have mistakenly thought that Merton's interest in the religions of the East somehow compromised his own Catholic faith and practice... The important truth is that Eastern spiritualities inspired Merton to deepen his understanding of, and commitment to, what could be discovered in the richness of his own native tradition in Christian mysticism.[3]

But the purpose here is not to debate what Merton might have been thinking as he neared the surprise of his own death or to speculate on that cryptic note he wrote as he boarded the plane for Bangkok, but to hopefully contribute, however minutely, to the meaning of Christian spirituality as something more than a set of abstract doctrinal propositions.

Although contemplation at the Abbey of Gethsemani was along the lines of medieval monastic *lectio divina,* Merton came to emphasize meditation more as described in the *Cloud of Unknowing*. The prayer of the heart, he said, "introduces us to deep interior silence so that we learn to experience its power. For that reason the prayer of the heart has to be always confined to the simplest acts and often making use of no words and no thoughts at all."[4]

As a graduate student at Columbia, Merton wrestled with whether he was called to be a Catholic monk, and if so, to what order and life. He felt his sense of contemplative vocation somehow affirmed by a verse in the Gospel of Luke: "Behold thou shalt be

---

2. Merton, *Love and Living,* 172, 183.
3. Merton, *Course in Christian Mysticism,* xii.
4. Merton, *Contemplative Prayer,* 42.

Contemplative Prayer and Contemporary Christianity

silent" (Luke 1:20 NASB)! Although a contemplative in this sense, Merton's appreciation of, and devotion to, other ways of praying, such as study, vocal prayer, *lectio divina,* and particularly the liturgy, were strong. Merton, as noted, wrote over sixty books and numerous articles, and his book *Contemplative Prayer* is an excellent place to begin to further explore the prayer of the heart.

MERTON—A COURSE ON CHRISTIAN MYSTICISM

A Course on Christian Mysticism is a book collection of selected lectures of Merton to the novices at the Abbey of Gethsemani. These lectures were meant to provide them with a spiritual, historical, and theological survey of Christian mysticism. The selected lectures, thirteen chapters, cover sixteen centuries from the Gospel of Saint John the Evangelist to Saint John of the Cross.

For many years, Thomas Merton was the novice master in the Abbey of Gethsemani, giving lectures, or conferences, to young men studying to become monks. The chapters in *A Course in Christian Mysticism,* represent some of his conferences given between 1961 and 1964. One day, returning to his cell after Lauds (the office said at daybreak), he was reflecting on the antiphon: "Hear and understand the instructions which God gave you." And he wrote in his journal, "We have no memory.... The loss of tradition is an important factor in the loss of contemplation."[5] I did not discover *A Course in Christian Mysticism* until nearly the very end of my own research for this little reflection, but the discovery has been a real joy. No small part of that joy was finding that Merton shared my concerns and aims—or rather that I shared his. Merton hoped to enhance the memory of the Christian contemplative tradition in young monastics, and in those responsible for their formation. He wanted them to see mysticism as central to not only monastic life, although certainly that, but also as central to all spiritual progress, and to the whole of life for every man and every woman of faith.

---

5. Merton, *Course in Christian Mysticism,* xiii.

In his introductory conference, Merton told the young monastics:

> Without mysticism there is no real theology, and without theology there is no real mysticism. Hence the emphasis will be on mysticism as theology, to bring out clearly the mystical dimensions of our theology, hence to help us to do what we must really do: live our theology. Some think it is sufficient to come to the monastery to live the Rule. More is required—we must live our theology, fully, deeply, in its totality. Without this, there is no sanctity. The separation of theology from "spirituality" is a disaster.[6]

In these lectures, Merton demonstrates how to bridge the gap between spirituality and academic theology, and in doing so shows his own depth and skill as a spiritual theologian.

The course begins with an exploration of the mystical foundations of the Gospel according to Saint John, and then moves forward to trace mystical theology through the centuries. Much of what is essential in Merton's own spiritual life can be heard in his lecture on John Tauler in which he says:

> Besides all the ordinary forms of self-love and attachment from which we must be purified, there is above all that self-will in the things of God, "wanting our own will to be carried out in all the things of God and even in God himself." This purification takes a long time.[7]

For Merton, in order to understand Christian mysticism, we must become serious about mystical union and the contemplative life of virtue, of self-denial, and of self-emptying quiet.

JOHN MAIN

John Main (1926–1982) was born in London with roots in County Kerry, Ireland. He was educated by the Jesuits. At the end of World War II, he served in the Royal Signal Corps. He joined the Canons

6. Ibid., 1.
7. Ibid., 158.

Regular of the Lateran and then left after a short stay to study law at Trinity College Dublin. He joined the British Diplomatic Service and was attached to the Governor General's Office in Malaya. Through his work he met an Indian monk and Justice of the Peace, Swami Satyanada. From him Main learned to meditate and began to practice silence, stillness, and simplicity as a part of his Christian faith. After returning, he continued his daily practice and taught international law at Trinity College. In 1958, he became a Benedictine monk in the Abbey in London. At Ealing he was asked to give up his meditation as something other than Christian prayer. However, as Headmaster at the school of Saint Anselm's Abbey in Washington D.C., he began to seriously study the roots of his Christian monastic tradition. In the Desert Fathers and Mothers, and in John Cassian, he found the Christian expression of the way of meditating he had learned in Malaya from the Swami. Main began to realize that this way of praying could be for many modern people what it had been for him, the way to a deeper experience, a more intense communion, with God. In 1975, he opened the first Christian Meditation Center at Ealing Abbey. The World Community for Christian Meditation now carries on the contemplative work of John Main under the direction of Father Lawrence Freeman. The work of John Main, and now the WCCM, is to be especially appreciated for its simple and straightforward approach.

THOMAS KEATING

The most successful effort to spread contemplative ideals and practice, at least in terms of sheer numbers, is probably the work of Thomas Keating and Contemplative Outreach, the organization he founded to further his work.

During the early to mid-sixties, Vatican II urged the religious orders to find ways of reviving the contemplative teachings of early Christianity and of making them available to those outside monasteries and convents. Near St. Joseph's Abbey in Spencer, Massachusetts, there was a Zen retreat center. Fathers Basil Pennington, Carl Menninger, and Thomas Keating began to realize that among those who would stop at the Abbey looking for directions to the Zen retreat center were many Roman Catholics. When they explored why this was so, they found that it was because people were drawn to the deep and beautiful silent practice of Zen meditation. Pennington, Menninger, and Keating then began to ask how they could make their monastic experience of contemplation available to laypeople. Apparently it was Pennington who suggested that *The Cloud of Unknowing* offered a simple method of contemplation—an imageless, wordless, quiet prayer of the heart. The monks then began to offer centering prayer workshops. The name may have been taken from Thomas Merton's description of contemplative prayer as prayer that is "centered entirely on the presence of God."[8] However, I remember Thomas Keating also saying that they had decided that so many people were wary of the word "contemplation" that "centering prayer" seemed the more useable term. In 1983, the organization Contemplative Outreach was formed to support the growing network of centering prayer practitioners.[9]

Centering prayer has often been criticized, generally unfairly, by people with a rather rigid and narrow understanding of what it means to pray as a Christian. Richard Foster once wrote, "Superficiality is the curse of our age."[10] Centering prayer has been highly instrumental in countering that curse, and for that, every person in the Christian community of faith should be enormously grateful.

CENTERING PRAYER

It is perhaps appropriate to take an ever so slight detour here to say something about centering prayer specifically. Robert Jonas, who is quite appreciative and supportive of Keating's work and of centering prayer, finds cause for some disagreement with Keating's concept of "unloading" (thoughts as psychological crap that need to be eliminated). Jonas asserts that Keating's approach is almost

8. Merton, *Contemplative Prayer*, 29–30.
9. Pennington, *Centering Prayer*.
10. Foster, *Celebration of Discipline*, 1.

Contemplative Prayer and Contemporary Christianity

exactly like Vipassana, insight Buddhist meditation. Both Vipassana meditation and Keating, Jonas thinks, find no spiritually significant difference between thoughts. In both, thoughts are just thoughts, memories just memories, and emotions mere emotions. But the reality is, Jonas goes on to say, that we cannot control how God will reach out to us.[11] I don't think Jonas is entirely correct in his understanding of Keating and centering prayer. Keating is not saying that every thought, emotion, or memory is crap to be eliminated, but that even if one experiences a deep insight while engaged in centering prayer, that is not the time to engage with it—let it go and explore it later. I think Jonas is correct in that we cannot control how God will reach out and connect with us; consequently, while sitting meditatively, we let go of analyzing or attending to our thoughts in any way, and in this way actually let go of our tendency to master and control.

Like Jonas, I also find a problem with the concept of unloading, but for an entirely different reason. I find it problematic in its nature as a concept, as a theoretical structure in a theoretical system of psychology. I am not entirely comfortable with the extent to which centering prayer has been turned into, or explained, as a psychological system rather than left as a simple way of prayer. This is much the same problem one finds in other proponents of centering prayer, such as Cynthia Bourgeault. The nineteenth-century English thinker, theologian, and activist priest, Frederick Denison Maurice, once said, "People are hungry for God and we give them a system."[12] That is the problem I see with centering prayer—it is just way too systematic and purports to explain way too much as a psychological theory.

Another difficulty I find with centering prayer, and this may be my Protestant training showing up, is that over the years it has increasingly framed itself as a way to contemplation rather than as contemplation itself. As I understand it, Roman Catholic theology as a system finds it necessary to distinguish between acquired contemplation and infused contemplation. However, neither the

---

11. Jonas, "Christian Prayer," 10.
12. Maurice, *Life of Frederick Denison Maurice*, 369.

ancient prophets of Israel nor the early Christians made such a distinction. Contemplation, or meditation, was one. While contemplating, one might reach a state of contemplation, or spiritual ecstasy, or quietude, or sense of being in the divine presence, or *Ruach HaKodesh*. No one word ever precisely describes it, but it is far less complicated than academic debates over whether contemplation is acquired or infused make it out to be.

Henri Nouwen spoke insightfully to this paradox of contemplation as both a gift and as something we do so as to participate in our own personal formation.

> The spiritual life is a gift. It is the gift of the Holy Spirit, who lifts us up into the kingdom of love. But to say that being lifted up into the kingdom of love is a divine gift does not mean we wait passively until the gift is offered to us. Jesus tells us to set our hearts on the kingdom. Setting our hearts on something involves not only serious aspiration but also strong determination. A spiritual life requires human effort.[13]

It seems to me this is in closer harmony with Scripture which moves comfortably back and forth between being "sanctified," to use the old word for becoming a holy or spiritual person, and participating in our own "sanctification."

This is not a huge problem. I just think Keating's tendency is to overly systematize and intellectualize—and therefore to complicate—meditative prayer, which by its very nature should be simple and straightforward, for simplicity is the essence of all contemplative prayer. Christianity, said T. S. Eliot, "is a condition of complete simplicity."[14]

HENRI J. M. NOUWEN

Henri J. M. Nouwen was one of the most popular writers of Christian spirituality in the twentieth century. He was born in Nijkerk,

---

13. Nouwen, *Making All Things New*, 65.
14. Eliot, "Little Gidding," in *Four Quartets*, 59.

Holland in 1932. Signifcant to his early years is that Holland was under Nazi occupation from the time Nouwen was eight until he was fourteen. He experienced a call to the priesthood at a young age and was ordained as a diocesan priest in the Archdiocese of Utrecht in 1957. He saw psychology as a way of exploring the human side of faith, both his own and the people he served, and so studied psychology at the Catholic University of Nijmegen. At Nijmegen, he was greatly influenced by Han Fortmann, a Dutch psychologist of religion whose writing about action and contemplation in a busy world finds numerous echoes in Nouwen's own work. After obtaining the *doctorandus* degree in 1964, he became a Fellow in the Religion and Psychiatry Program at the Menninger Clinic in Topeka, Kansas. At the Menninger Clinic, Nouwen discovered he was far more interested in direct contact with patients than in scientific and medical analysis. By training, by compassion, and by call, then, Nouwen was essentially a pastoral theologian. He taught pastoral theology for twenty years, first at the University of Notre Dame, and then at the Yale and Harvard Divinity Schools. He was immensely popular with students. He was also a prolific writer. Seven million copies of his books in multiple languages were sold. His writing was focused primarily on spirituality in the practice of ministry. The contemplative character of his many books is obvious in their simplicity of style and depth of insight. Nouwen let go of the status and prestige that went with being a Harvard professor, and went to L'Arche Daybreak in Ontario to work with mentally and physically handicapped people. For several months during the 1970s, Nouwen lived and worked with the Trappist monks in the Abbey of the Genesee, and in the early 1980s lived with the poor in Peru. Both experiences were profoundly formative for him. The truth is that there does not seem to be much in Herni Nouwen's experience that he did not find to be useful material for his own spiritual formation and that he did not make available for the healing and spiritual transformation of others.

Nouwen's teaching on contemplative prayer is, in many instances, more indirect than direct. While he did not write much on contemplation as a technique, he was quite explicit about the need to practice silence and solitude. He said, "Without solitude it is virtually impossible to live a spiritual life. Solitude begins with a time and place for God, and him alone."[15] "In solitude," he thought, "our hearts become like quiet cells where God can dwell, wherever we go and whatever we do."[16]

It is interesting to notice in this regard that both Nouwen and Thomas Merton wrote books on the spirituality of the desert monks, and that each felt simple words and phrases like "prayer of silence" or "rest" were more descriptive of their spiritual practice than "contemplation." In writing of the Desert Fathers, Merton said:

> When Arsenius is told to fly from the Cenobium, be silent and rest (*fuge, tace,* quiesce) it is a call to "contemplative prayer." *Quies* is a simpler and less pretentious term than "contemplation," and much less misleading. It suits the simplicity of the Desert Fathers much better than "contemplation," and affords less occasion for narcissism and megalomania.[17]

Nouwen's spiritual theology was even less complex than Merton's. It was simple, intelligent, profound, and immensely practical.

When people read Nouwen's books or heard him teach or speak, his words resonated deep within them. He thought of spiritual theology and contemplation as a spirituality of the heart. By "the heart" Nouwen meant our true self or the totality of our being—our soul, spirit, heart, and mind, our solid, real self, or whatever you want to call it. In *Letters to Marc* he wrote:

> Self-knowledge, and self-love are the fruits of knowing and loving God. . . Laying our hearts totally open to God leads to a love of ourselves that enables us to give wholehearted love to our fellow human beings. In the seclusion of our hearts we learn to know the hidden presence of

---

15. Nouwen, *Making All Things New*, 69.
16. Ibid., 79.
17. Merton, *Wisdom of the Desert*, 20.

Contemplative Prayer and Contemporary Christianity

God; and with that spiritual knowledge we can lead a loving life.[18]

Nouwen thought that the heart is more knowledgeable than the mind. We must, therefore, learn to follow the practice of the Eastern Orthodox Christian mystics of allowing the heart to descend into the mind which, in the end, is the practice of solitude and silence, the practice of, to use what he thought of as that overly complicated word, "contemplation."

For Nouwen, contemplative prayer, the spirituality of the heart, was inseparable from a strong theology of peace and social justice. Like Thomas Merton, the deeper he went spiritually, the further out his compassion for others extended. Some of the more obvious signs of his identification with the purpose of God include his marching for civil rights, serving the poor in Latin America, working with the handicapped members of the L'Arche community, and his service to victims of AIDS. Nouwen believed that the compassionate life, which is the life of Christ, is the life of "downward mobility."[19] In a society in which upward mobility is the ideal, downward mobility appears foolish, stupid, and even crazy. Yet, it is in downward mobility that life that really is life is discovered as we pray the prayer of the open heart.

---

18. Nouwen, *Letters to Mark*, 75.
19. Nouwen, *Selfless Way of Christ*, 39.

SIX

Some Final Observations

I have suggested many ways of praying, and perhaps you have noted that sooner or later they all lead to silence wherein you rest in the presence of God. The old theologians expressed this by saying that all forms of prayer converge finally on contemplative prayer. No matter where you begin, you end with contemplation. And so whenever you enter into this loving silence and deep peace, stay there. Remain in the silence until (as may well happen) you get overwhelmed with distractions: then return to the repetition of your word or phrase until it once more leads you into silence. In contemplative prayer there is an interplay of words and silence. As time goes on you will find the words rise out of the silence, and silence rises out of the words. Silence is valuable. But do not make a fetish out of silence, and do not make a fetish of words. What matters is neither silence nor words but faith and love.

WILLIAM JOHNSTON[1]

---

1. Johnston, *Being in Love*, 41.

Some Final Observations

IN THE LIST OF CONTEMPLATIVES

THERE ARE MANY OTHER important figures in the history of meditation, of contemplation, that could have been, and maybe even should have been, noted.

Saint Augustine (354–430 CE), whose episcopacy in North Africa ran nearly parallel to the early part of the monastic movement, was both a classical scholar—indeed, some say the last of the classical scholars—and if such a term can be used, a classical mystic. His *Confessions* speak of a wordless hearing of the divine *logos,* of being transported to a place of "unlikeness," and of his heart filling with divine light. Augustine is particularly interesting in that while he can be enrolled among the greatest of mystics, he lived quite an active life as both a scholar and church leader. In a reflection on Psalms 34:7–8, Augustine has a wonderful and inviting description of meditation as an interior experience of seeking nothing but communion with God, nothing (no-thing) but the simple and humble presence of Christ:

> "I sought the Lord and he heard me." Where did the Lord hear me? Within. Where did he respond to me? Within. There you pray, there you are heard, you are blessed and one who stands right next to you knows nothing of this. It is all carried on in secret, just as the Lord instructs our prayer in the Gospel telling us to enter our special private place and when we have shut the door, to pray to our Father in secret; and our Father, who sees what we do in secret, will reward us openly (Matt. 6:6). When you enter your room, you are entering your heart. The Psalmist did not say, I sought gold from the Lord, and he heard me, or I sought long life from the Lord, and he heard me, or I sought whatever, this or that, from the Lord, and he heard me. It is one thing to seek anything from the Lord, and another to seek the Lord himself. "I sought the Lord," the Psalmist says, "and he heard me." Therefore do not seek from the Lord anything in the outside world; just seek the Lord himself and he will hear you and even while you are still speaking, he will say, "Yes. Here I am."[2]

2. Ulanov, *Prayers of St. Augustine,* 134–35.

Gregory the Great (540–604 CE) was descended from Roman nobles and a family which had provided the church with strong leadership. He was related to Popes Felix III and Agapitus I. His aunts were nuns, and his parents joined cloisters in their later years. Gregory was well educated, and by age thirty he was the chief administrative officer of Rome, responsible for finances, police, provisioning, and public works. He used his experience, wealth, and position to create six monasteries.

When his father died in 574, Gregory converted his house into a monastery and retired to a life of contemplation and prayer. These years of contemplation and detailed Bible study were the happiest in Gregory's life.

In 577, Pope Benedict appointed Gregory one of the seven deacons of Rome, and a little later Pope Pelagius II made him his confidential adviser. In 589, a flood destroyed the grain reserves of Rome, resulting first in famine and then a plague epidemic. Pope Pelagius himself died as a victim of the plague that swept through Rome. Gregory was then elected to succeed him.

Gregory was passionate about the work of priests. He wrote a book of instruction for bishops, *On Pastoral Rule*, which remained in use for centuries as a manual of pastoral care in the Western Church. "The ruler" (bishop), he wrote, "should be a near neighbor to everyone in sympathy, and exalted above all in contemplation." By "loving-kindness," he thought, priests would be able to "transfer the infirmities" of others to themselves, and by the "loftiness of contemplation transcend themselves in their aspiration after the invisible."[3]

Gregory's contemplation of Scripture led him to see it as ". . . a door which provides an entrance into invisible truths. . . . a cool forest in which we find shelter from the world's burning heat"; and, ". . . a river, shallow and deep in which lambs can wade and elephants swim."[4] Gregory certainly believed that the Bible should be read academically and for intellectual understanding, but he also thought it must be read with an openness to conversion, and with a

---

3. Gregory I, *Book of Pastoral Rule*, 19–20.
4. McGinn, *Growth of Christian Mysticism*, 40.

Some Final Observations

poetic sense that leads to an understanding of the spiritual life, for "Scripture is a mountain to be climbed—thick with meaning and covered with allegories." He imagined the Bible as "a flint stone from which the fire of spiritual understanding can be struck."[5] He said that those who know nothing of celestial contemplation, and are hemmed in by the darkness of this world, are the truly blind.[6] Bernard McGinn says, "For Gregory, as for the Latin Fathers in general, the qualifier *mysticus* refers almost exclusively to the hidden, deeper sense of scripture."[7]

Significantly, McGinn notes that while Gregory wrote no treatise on contemplation, he really did not need to do so since it is there throughout his work. The four features of contemplation found in Gregory are easily seen as those characteristics of the practice of mystical presence discussed throughout this short history:

1) The human person was created to contemplate the creator, always seeking God's beauty in the solemnity of Christ's love.

2) The Christian has access to the contemplative vision of God through Christ who connects the outer and the inner—connects contemplation with action.

3) Contemplation is simply attentive regard for God alone.

4) All Christians are called to contemplation.

Gregory believed that in this life it is possible for Christians to experience the vision of God, that in contemplation it is possible for us to enter the region of awe where we experience the mystery of God as the chief glory of our lives and the fulfillment of the deepest and truest desire of our hearts.

The Keepers (600–1000 CE) of the contemplative and mystical tradition of Christianity for the next four to five hundred years following Gregory were primarily the monasteries. "There are," Bernard McGinn notes, "no outstanding mystical authors in the

---

5. Ibid., 10.
6. Gregory I, *Book of Pastoral Rule*, 10.
7. McGinn, *Growth of Christian Mysticism*, 141.

early medieval period."[8] However, during this time the monasteries and convents were the primary keepers and transmitters of the Christian spiritual tradition of contemplation, of mysticism as the presence of God and Christ's love.

Monastic spirirtuality during this time, at least in general, shared certain common disciplines and characteristics:

Oratio is "word-filled" prayer. It may be a short prayer at the beginning of sacred reading or meditation expressing desire and longing for God's presence. Or after a Scripture reading, after having heard God's word. It is the natural response emerging from wonder, love, and gratitude, or it may be a praying of the verse read so that the language of Scripture becomes what it already is—the language of prayer.

Solitude as an abandonment or renunciation of the world—of its values and ways of understanding. In fact, the question became whether that could be done apart from a monastic life.

Silence, what was known as the *competens silentium*, "the fitting silence," which is an attentiveness to God that leads to an absolute quiet and rest in the love, presence, power, and mystery of God.

Reading as *lectio divina* involved reading Scripture out loud, since speaking and hearing together involve more of the whole person, and reading with reflective pauses with the intent and willingness to absorb the inner meaning and beauty of the text. McGinn quotes Smaragdus:

> It often happens that someone can grasp that the words of sacred scripture are mystical if that person himself, enflamed by the grace of heavenly contemplation, hangs upon things celestial. The marvelous and inexpressible power of the sacred text is acknowledged when the reader's intellectual soul is penetrated by love from on high.[9]

Meditatio is the slow repetition, often audibly, of a text—ruminating on a single word of expression, turning it over and over

---

8. Ibid., 119.
9. Ibid., 134.

Some Final Observations

again and allowing it to sink into the depths of our being, and there to be absorbed so that we become one with it. The reading of any text is complete only when we have become one with the word.

Contemplatio occurs when all words, images, and concepts fall away and prayer becomes the gift of quiet stillness in the presence of God. Some have imagined all of these elements as a movement in which one moves gently and naturally from vocal prayer to contemplation.

Through these spiritual practices, then, the monks and nuns in the monasteries and convents of early medieval Christianity kept and nourished the ancient mystical and contemplative tradition of Christianity.

In fact, the monastic contemplative tradition of the Middle Ages has been kept to our present day without interruption. Contemplation has, for example, now been a central practice of the Cistercians for a thousand years. In the eleventh century, three monks departed from Molesme Abbey in France to found the first Cistercian monastery, Citeaux Abbey. The Order quickly grew when Saint Bernard of Clairvaux, who is known as the spiritual father of the Cistercians, entered the monastery in 1112 and convinced some thirty friends and relatives to join him. The Cistercians are a cloistered order. The monks seek to maintain a stable community, a "school of brotherly love," as they call it, in which simplicity, silence (speaking only when necessary), and profound quiet even in the performance of work and necessary tasks creates an atmosphere which nourishes classical contemplation. Trappist monks are those Cistercians who are the more exacting and strict in the observance of their rule. One way to keep from getting confused is to remember that all Trappists are Cistercians, but all Cistercians are not Trappists.

Hildegard of Bingen (1098–1179 CE) was, from the time she was a very young girl, a person of mystical visions. She said she first saw "The Shade of the Living Light" at the age of three, and by the age of five understood that she was experiencing visions. She believed her visions to be a gift from God which she could not explain to others.

Hildegard was a brilliant woman who wrote extensively. Her literary work includes the lives of saints and two treatises on medicine and natural history. The latter shows a quality of scientific observation which is rare for that time. She engaged in extensive correspondence which contains a number of allegorical treatises. For amusement she created her own language. Her guidance and advice were frequently sought in ecclesiastical and religious matters. She was declared a Doctor of the Church and a Saint after her death.

Much of Saint Hildegard's mystical thought found expression in her musical compositions, plays, and poetry. One of my favorite poems of hers is "Holy Spirit," which I have translated below:

> Holy Spirit, life giving life,
> animating all,
> root of all
> cleansing the soul,
> purifying the heart,
> healing wounds.
> You are luminous and wonderful,
> reviving the spirit,
> awakening all from sleep.

Julian of Norwich (1342–1416 CE), was an anchoress and mystic. Her *Revelation of Divine Love* is the first book in the English language known to have been written by a woman. As an anchoress, Julian set herself apart for God and lived a solitary life, much like a religious hermit, in confined quarters called an anchorage—a single small cell or walled-in room attached to a church. Julian became known in her own time as a wise spiritual director, and gave counsel from a window in her anchorage

Before becoming an anchoress at the age of 32, Julian became seriously ill and had what we would probably think of as a near-death experience. She received a series of sixteen visions.[10] Her *Revelation of Divine Love* is an explanation and reflection on her visions. The two that most people are aware of are Christ saying to her with great compassion in her weakness and suffering as she

---

10. McGinn, *Essential Writings of Christian Mysticism*, 238–242.

Some Final Observations

received the Last Rites: "And all shall be well. And all shall be well. And all manner of things shall be exceeding well."[11] The second is her explanation of the essence of the sixteen "showings" as she called them.

After many years of reflecting on her original vision she was given this spiritual understanding. "Would you know your Lord's meaning in this thing?" she asked or was asked.

> Know it well, love was his meaning. Who showed it to you? Love. What did he show you? Love. Why did he show it? For love. Keep yourself therein and you shall know and understand more in the same. But you shall never know nor understand any other thing, forever.[12]

From this revelation of love Julian found it natural to be joyful in all circumstances for no matter how great the adversity, in Christ we cannot be overcome, and ultimately all things will be put right by Christ.

Her experience of the love of Christ was of something so gentle, so caring, so motherly, that she referred to Jesus as "Christ our Mother." "Truth," she said, "sees God, and wisdom contemplates God, and from these two comes a third, a holy and wonderful delight in God, who is love."[13] That, I think, is a wonderful explanation of contemplative prayer.

Therese of Lisieux (1873–1897 CE), entered the Carmel of Lisieux with the determination to become a saint, but six years as a Carmelite left her with the realization that she and her own efforts were far too small and insignificant. In terms of classical Christian spirituality and contemplation, we can think of this as the self-emptying of Philippians which is necessary for the mystical life to flourish. Therese saw how very far she was from the unfailing practice of Christ's love. One day while meditating on the Old Testament she was grasped in her reading by Proverbs 9:6 which says, "Whosoever is a little one, let him come to me." Then, on another

---

11. Armstrong, *Visions of God*, 193.

12. Julian of Norwich, *Revelations of Divine Love*, 40, 41, 45, 60, 99, 100, 124–25.

13. Ibid., 77–78, 100–2.

occasion, she was mesmerized by Isaiah 66:12–13: "You shall be carried at the breasts, and upon the knees they shall caress you. As one whom the mother caresseth, so will I comfort you." She saw that the spiritual path lies along the lines of what we have heard Nouwen call the path of "downward mobility."[14]

What Therese called "the little way"[15] is the foundation of her spirituality. I cannot help but think when reading of Saint Therese of something William James once wrote:

> I am done with great things and big things, great institutions and big success, and I am for those tiny, invisible molecular moral forces that work from individual to individual, creeping through the crannies of the world like so many rootlets, or like the capillary oozing of water, yet which if you give them time, will rend the hardest monuments of human pride.[16]

Or as Saint Theresa of Calcutta often reminded us, "It is not the size of the gift that matters most, but the love in it." This is the way of contemplative practice and wisdom, *la petite voie*.

What Saint Therese discovered was that all personal ambitions, even quite holy ones (like the desire for sainthood), work against the contemplative life—like rowing upstream or attempting to sail into the wind. Karl Rahner thought that one of the utterly amazing, and to us sometimes quite confusing, things about the life of Jesus is that it was framed within everyday life. In Christ we discover the joy of a "mysticism of daily life."[17]

While the little way is absolute simplicity it is unfathomable. Therese had a vision in which she saw Christ bruised, battered, and bloodied. His tears and blood fell to the ground but there was no one to gather them up, meaning no one really cared or noticed. This becomes then the spirituality of the little way; that

---

14. Nouwen, *Selfless Way of Christ*, 39.

15. Therese of Lisieux, *Story of a Soul*, xi. Also St. Therese of Lisieux, *The Little Way for Everyday*, 63, 66–67, 77–79.

16. Quoted in Clinebell Jr., *Basic Types of Pastoral Counseling*, 57.

17. Egan, *Karl Rahner*, 55–79.

Some Final Observations

is, to be one who sees those who weep and bleed, especially the little-noticed and unwanted, and to care.

Evelyn Underhill (1875–1941 CE), was an English Anglo-Catholic mystic, author, and pacifist. She was one of the most widely read writers on Christian mysticism and spiritual practice in the first half of the twentieth century. Her best-known work is probably *Mysticism*, published in 1911.

Underhill defined the life of prayer as "our whole life toward heaven." No matter what type of prayer you pray, she insisted, it is communion with God. The work of real prayer, she thought, "is a great and difficult art." The spiritual life, she said, like our physical life, requires food, a steady diet of reading Scripture and the spiritual classics; fresh air, living with an attitude of wonder and gratitude; and, it requires exercise, a disciplined routine of spiritual practice. She thought that "adoration," and "adherence" are the ways we prepare for the mystical or spiritual life. They are not the spiritual life itself, but the way in which we prepare for it. Adoration is the attitude which places God, and not one's self, at the center of life. Adherence is being passionately devoted to our relationship with God so that it takes precedence over all other things. For Underhill, the mystical or contemplative life means we live every moment in recognition that we are in the intimate presence of God.[18]

C. S. Lewis (1898–1963 CE) was a British novelist, poet, academic, medievalist, literary critic, essayist, lay theologian, broadcaster, lecturer, and Christian apologist. He held academic positions at both Oxford and Cambridge Universities. He is best known for his works of fiction—especially *The Screwtape Letters*, *The Chronicles of Narnia*, and *The Space Trilogy*—and for his non-fiction Christian apologetics such as *Mere Christianity*, *Miracles*, and *The Problem of Pain*.

Lewis and fellow novelist J. R. R. Tolkien were close friends. They both served on the English faculty at Oxford University and were active in the informal Oxford literary group known as the

---

18. Johnson, "Life as Prayer," 1–11. See also Evelyn Underhill's books, *Mysticism*, and *Spiritual Life*.

Inklings. According to Lewis's *Surprised By Joy*, his conversion to the Christian faith as an adult had a great deal to do with the influence of Tolkien, a devout Catholic, as well as other literary friends.

While Lewis was widely known and cited as a Christian intellectual, not many are aware of his profound Christian mysticism. For example, in *Surprised by Joy*, his little memoir, he wrote of his Christian conversion like this:

> Into the region of awe, in deepest solitude there is a road right out of the self, a commerce with. . . the naked other, imageless (though our imaginations salute it with a hundred images), unknown, undefined, desired.[19]

Only someone who is a true mystic and experienced in the wonder of contemplative prayer, the prayer of solitude, could write such lines.

While *Bede Griffith* (1906–1993 CE) remained a Roman Catholic priest his whole life and died a Benedictine monk, his attempts to connect Christian mysticism with Hinduism led in some troubling theological directions, and for that reason his work has not been emphasized here where the intent has been to show the rich contemplative tradition of a Christian spirituality that is quite at home in the large house of theological orthodoxy. Nevertheless, he remains an important figure among modern Christian mystics and in the connective history of Christian contemplative practice.[20]

Martin Thornton (1915–1986 CE), an Anglican priest and spiritual director, wrote with a style that is now perhaps a little dated, but nevertheless still has much wisdom to offer, especially in developing a rule of life.[21] Many have also found his writings on prayer enormously helpful.

Thornton's formal education was initally in the field of agriculture, and in fact he began his adult life as a farmer on land which his father acquired and which Thornton himself managed.

---

19. Lewis, *Surprised by Joy*, 221.

20. It is for this same reason I have not discussed Meister Eckhart or the Rhineland mystics in these pages.

21. Thornton, *Christian Proficiency*.

Some Final Observations

He is credited with developing an innovative style of ploughing, and with adopting what are now thought of as sustainable or organic farming practices. In *My God: A Reappraisal of Normal Religious Experience*, Thornton describes a mystical experience, an experience of the *numinous*, as he walked in the field one day reflecting on his own direction in life:

> It was mid-November, dark, dank, negative, and I walked through a swamp and across two meadows.... Then the fog descended, and so did the Spirit, all-shrouding is better than all-enveloping, because the former word hints at death while the latter has the false (in this case) connotation of comforting protection. If you want to make shallow jests about omnipresence and holy fog, then go ahead; I shall not be amused, nor shall I be abashed. The presence of God was disclosed through the total foggy environment; and the disclosure pointed to the Father transcendent....[22]

Thornton thought that it was laypeople rather than the professional theologians who were most likely to experience the mysterious presence of God. He said that members of the church have become like a bunch of professors who all enjoy eating popcorn in private, but who won't admit it to one another because that would be undignified.

Thornton graduated from Queens College in 1946, and was ordained in the Church of England in 1947. What Thornton wanted to do was to teach people to pray. He wanted ordinary Christians to grasp the richness, the spiritual profundity, and the humility of life in Christ. He believed that the primary pastoral need today is for competent spiritual direction in the contemplative life.

William Johnston (1925–2010 CE), Catholic priest, scholar, Jesuit, and mystic who was based at Sophia University in Japan until his death, was an authority on *The Cloud of Unknowing* and connected Zen insights to Christian meditation in a way that enriched Christian spiritual theology while remaining genuinely

---

22. Thornton, *My God*, 95–97.

orthodox.[23] In *Silent Music: The Science of Meditation*, he explored the concept of meditation from multiple perspectives—religious, psychological, spiritual, and scientific. In *Silent Music*, Johnston showed a helpful way of understanding mysticism, contemplation, and our search for wisdom in the modern world.

And *Martin Laird*, who currently teaches at Villanova University, is more than a little helpful as a contemplative guide. His book, *Into the Silent Land: A Guide to the Christian Practice of Contemplation*, is a wonderful book for those just beginning to explore the contemplative path.

There are so very many more in the list of contemplatives (Catherine of Siena, Frederick von Hugel, Simone Weil), and we have not really touched the luxuriant fabric of Eastern Orthodox spirituality, nor traced the providence of its mystical tradition, but these few are given here in chapters six and seven to furnish the linkage of Christian mysticism and the practice of contemplative prayer with all the generations of our spiritual ancestors.[24]

ABOUT THE DISTINCTION OF WORDS

I should, no doubt, have indicated at the beginning that although contemplation and meditation do not actually mean the same thing I have used them interchangeably here. In the East, the word "meditation" denotes what we mean by "contemplation." And the word "contemplation" is what we have traditionally meant by "meditation." Whatever the terminology, what I have been concerned with here is nondiscursive prayer and those practices that, no matter how active at first, lead one into a prayer beyond words, thoughts, concepts, and images. William Johnston's comments are especially worth noting:

---

23. Johnston, *Silent Music*. See also Johnston, *Lord Teach Us to Pray*.

24. For those more comfortable with a strongly Protestant evangelical perpsective, I would suggest E. Stanley Jones's *The Way*; W. E. Sangster's *The Secret of Radiant Life*; James Stewart's *A Man in Christ*, Richard Foster's *Celebration of Discipline*, and Dallas Willard's *The Spirit of the Discipines*.

Some Final Observations

> In the meditation of the great religions one makes progress by going beyond thought, beyond concepts, beyond images, beyond reasoning, thus entering a deeper state of consciousness or enhanced awareness that is characterized by profound silence. This is the *silentium mysticum*. It is the state of consciousness in which there may be no words or images. . . .This book (*Silent Music*), then, is about meditation. Let me say, however, that the choice of this word has caused me some anguish. I use it in the widest possible sense to include discursive thinking and reasoning about ultimate matters as well as what Christians call *contemplation* and Hindus call *Samadhi* and Buddhists *Zen*. In it I also include mysticism—which in my opinion, is no more than a very deep form of meditation. It was difficult to find an all-embracing word that would include these disparate things, and it seemed to me that "meditation" was the best. For me, meditation, in the last analysis, is the search for wisdom, or the relishing of wisdom when it has been found.[25]

Our spiritual fathers and mothers obviously did not make all the fine distinctions between prayer, meditation, and contemplation that seem to matter so much to us. Better to experience the mysterious presence of God in prayer than to learnedly and theoretically discuss it. Thomas Merton thought that when we perceive a conflict in the types of prayer there is a kind of dislocation that results. "But in the early monastic tradition," he says, "there was no such division, no such conflict. The whole life of the monk is considered as 'praying always.'"[26]

I certainly hope that my own more narrow focus on contemplation as the holy silence of a quiet heart and mind and body, the stillness of wordless and imageless prayer, in no way leaves the impression that I am dismissing the importance of other forms of prayer, such as vocal prayer, liturgical prayer, the praying of Scripture, reciting or chanting the Psalms, the practice of sacramental spirituality, the singing of hymns as prayer, or the mental

---

25. Johnston, *Silent Music*, 10, 55. Also see Hart, *Alleluia is the Song*, iv–xvi.
26. Merton, *Contemplative Prayer*, 31.

reflection on things good, beautiful, and true. William Barry, in his book *God and You,* tells about a wonderful conversation he had with his mother about prayer not long before she died. Father Barry's mother had told him she wished God would take her in her sleep. Barry asked his mother what God is like, and she answered, "God is a lot better than what he's made out to be." Barry then goes on to say:

> How did she learn about God? Not because of books because my mother read very little. It was simply from praying a lot. And the prayers she said were mostly the rosary and devotions, prayer forms not much in favor these days. One time I asked her what happened when she prayed. During her response she said something like this: "Sometimes when you're saying your prayers, you go deep and you know he's listening to you and you to him." Apparently my mother had gotten to know the living God and found him a good deal more benign than he had been made out to be.[27]

I do have to admit that I have at times wondered, after reading this story, if the simple prayers William Barry's mother prayed did not lead her into contemplation in its more mystical sense.

A FINAL WORD ABOUT INTENTIONS

Another thing that may have perhaps been better said back at the beginning is that my intention was not to survey the great contemplatives, but rather to trace the ancestral trajectory of contemplative practice sufficiently to first help those of the Christian faith appreciate and value their contemplative spiritual heritage, and second, to provide something of an antidote to those who are afraid that meditation is less than Christian. George A. Lane's words in *Christian Spirituality: An Historical Sketch* are appropriate here:

---

27. Barry, *God and You,* 16.

> We should have a positive attitude, a respect for genuine mysticism. But where does one find genuine mysticism? The attitude of the Church has always been one of extreme caution in this regard. Perhaps this should be our attitude too, caution and respect, while at the same time we acknowledge the immense good that has come to the church from the authentic mystics.[28]

Having repeated Lane's caution, I must add that I personally have found nothing particularly dangerous in contemplative prayer.

Obviously, anyone already suffering from a mental disorder who finds meditation anxiety-provoking should stop what they are doing immediately and consult with a qualified therapist. Although one would expect, even here, that it is more likely that quieting the heart, mind, and body will prove therapeutic rather than disorienting. It might be helpful to read Part III of William Johnston's book *Silent Music*, which deals in four very short chapters with "Healing,"[29] or my own *A Little Book of Sanity: Finding Serenity in the Age of Anxiety*.[30]

Very conservative Christians are sometimes advised that contemplation will leave them open to dark and demonic forces. That sort of advice is based almost entirely on irrational fear and a need to control. M. Scott Peck, the well-known psychiatrist and author, noted in his book on evil that his own firsthand studies indicated one cannot be possessed by "demonic forces" against his or her will, but that the individual must in some sense first "sell out." Peck, who came to believe in "personal" evil and possession only after he began researching and writing his book, said:

> I would conclude that possession is no accident. I very much doubt that somebody can go walking down the street one day and have a demon jump out from behind a bush and penetrate him. Possession appears to be a

---

28. Lane, *Christian Spirituality*, 42–44.
29. Johnston, *Silent Music*, 107–38.
30. Hart, *Little Book of Sanity*.

gradual process in which the possessed person repeatedly sells out for one reason or another.[31]

This is the very opposite of genuine mystical contemplation in which, by being open to the presence of God, one discovers that none of the things we fear are anything to fear.

Actually, the greatest danger of contemplative prayer is that we will be tempted to practice what Thomas Merton referred to as a kind of "pseudomysticism" in which, rather than discovering authentic communion with God through surrender and renunciation, we center instead upon the "individualistic enjoyment of experience."[32]

So, to reiterate, contemplation and/or meditation is a prayer of love, it is a being in love, and we cannot be in love, we cannot consecrate our hearts and minds to the love of Christ and others, and at the same time be self-absorbed, or in darkness. We cannot be in the prayer of simply being in the presence of the Holy Trinity and simultaneously exist subject to fear and confusion. But, if the idea of letting go, of emptying yourself in order to be filled with the mystery of God's divine presence makes you nervous, then as will be suggested in chapter seven, surround your contemplation with verbal prayer and Scripture and you will grow in skill and confidence. But the most important thing is that you give yourself wholeheartedly to those prayer forms to which the Spirit draws you.

---

31. Peck, *People of the Lie*, 190.
32. Merton, *Love and Living*, 77–78.

SEVEN

It's Easier Than You Think

We enter the land of silence by the silence of surrender, and there is no map of the silence that is surrender. There are skills, however, by which we learn to dispose ourselves to surrender and thus discover this uncharted land. Moreover, there is the communal support of fellow pilgrims living and dead, whose wisdom comes to us in countless writings and through innumerable acts of compassion and who teach us what it means to "walk by faith, not by sight" (2 Cor 5:7).

MARTIN LAIRD[1]

THE SILENT LAND

CONTEMPLATIVE PRAYER IS PRAYER which contains no words, or thoughts or images. As previously noted, "contemplation" and "meditation" have reverse meanings in the East and West. In Eastern thought, meditation refers to this nondiscursive sort of prayer, and contemplation refers to pondering or thinking about something, whereas in the Western world, meditation has to do

---

1. Laird, *Into the Silent Land*, 3.

with reflecting on something in one's own mind, mentally turning it over again and again, and contemplation refers to sitting without images, thoughts, or words. Sometimes contemplative prayer is called the prayer of silence, the prayer of the heart, the prayer of loving attention, or centering prayer. Contemplation is sitting silently in the presence of God. In this prayer, we are not seeking insight, searching for answers, or reaching for conclusions. We are not trying to make anything happen, nor are we trying to keep anything from happening. We relinquish all efforts to control our world. No analysis takes place. If you have an amazing insight during contemplative prayer you let it go—think about it, ponder it, analyze it later. Contemplative prayer is nonconceptual prayer. We do not ask for anything. We are not looking for an experience, or trying to achieve enlightenment. Our one loving intention is to be with God. The anonymous medieval Christian mystic who authored *The Cloud of Unknowing* and the *Book of Privy Counselling* provides this instruction:

> When thou comest by thyself think not before what thou shalt do after but forsake as well good thoughts as evil thoughts. And pray not with thy mouth... And look that nothing remain in thy mind but a naked intent stretching unto God, not clothed in any special thought of God in himself, how he is in himself, but that God is as he is.[2]

When this author speaks of *naked intent,* he is speaking of an act of love. William Johnson explains that in authentic Christian contemplation there is a movement of unrestricted and unconditional love at the core of one's being. When you sit in loving emptiness, loving silence, loving awareness, you are not just practicing a prayer of being, but a prayer of being in love.[3] This is what makes Christian meditation or contemplation different from other traditions.

2. Johnston, *Mysticism of the Cloud*, 39.
3. Johnston, *Being in Love*, 82.

It's Easier Than You Think

THE LARGER PATTERN

My suggestion is that you incorporate contemplative prayer into the pattern of your larger devotional practice. For example, you might meditate on Scripture, that is follow the practice of *lectio divina*. To practice *lectio divina*: select a Scripture passage which is not too long, and not too short.[4] Read through it quickly once or twice so that you have a good overview. Now go back and begin to read slowly, rhythmically, reflectively. The words should be spaced far enough apart in your reading that you can attend to them, but not so far apart that they no longer work together to form meaning. When you find yourself drawn to a particular word or phrase do not go on reading the rest of the text. Repeat that word or phrase over and over again so that it falls inward, sinking deeper and deeper into you. Stay with that word or phrase as long, and for as many sittings, as it draws you in. You could let ten or fifteen minutes of *lectio divina* then draw you into twenty minutes of contemplation.

Whether you incorporate *lectio divina* or not, you will probably want to bracket your wordless contemplation with simple prayer or colloquy on both ends. In this way you move from prayer, to sacred reading, into contemplation, and emerge with verbal prayer to conclude.

CENTERING DOWN

You will certainly need some sort of centering down exercise. It is helpful to have a space set aside for silent prayer that is as free as possible from noise and distractions, a place that feels safe, and which maybe you can consecrate as a personal holy place, a place of prayer. You might want a little table of some sort with a candle (electric if you are as careless as I am) on it and maybe a cross, incense burner, a prayer book or Bible. Make sure you are sitting comfortably enough not to be distracted by physical annoyances,

---

4. The passage should have universal appeal; examples might include, Psalms 23; 27; 29; or 141; Matthew 5:1–10, 11–16; 6:19–34; Colossians 3:1–17.

but not so comfortable as to encourage sleepiness. It is best not to attempt contemplative prayer right after a meal—the tendency to drowsiness is just too great. You want to be both relaxed and alert, calm and attentive. Whatever sitting position you choose, it is important to keep the back straight. Close your eyes lightly as a way of letting go of what is going on around and within you. Some people, especially when they first begin this type of practice, find it helpful to imagine themselves softly floating down, deeper and deeper, down into that solitary place where they feel completely alone with God. Let your breath be slow, deep, and regular. Your breath may slow down till it almost seems to stop. You may want to begin each time by taking a deep breath and holding it for a moment before exhaling slowly or take a deep breath and then sigh it all out. Do this four or five times. This is a good way to signal a transition in your work and in your intention. As you are doing all of this let go of all thinking, that means all mental chatter in your mind, all fantasies, sense perceptions, pictures, reflections, and ideas.

LETTING GO OF THOUGHTS

What you will discover immediately is that it is extremely difficult to be completely still in body, mind, and heart. The body can be restless and break the silence to tell us of every itch, twitch, or discomfort. The mind can wander quick and far in its imaginations, questioning, philosophizing, engaging in remembrances and self-evaluations, like "How am I doing in my prayer?" Do not fight thinking, or exert force of will against it, or judge it since this is to take the bait and struggle on the hook of distraction. When I was a boy living in the country, my dog, a German Shepherd/Coyote mix, would chase jackrabbits. He was a fast runner and could have caught lots of rabbits if they had only run in a straight line. But alas jackrabbits don't run in a straight line. They change direction suddenly. They zig and zag. That dog could chase a rabbit for, what at least seemed to me as a boy, a long time and over great distances without ever catching it. It could be a good while before he finally made it back home, exhausted and without any rabbit. That's what it's like chasing thoughts in our mind. So just gently notice your thoughts and let them drift away.

I think it is the Eastern spiritual writer Eknath Easwaran who said the only way to have a blank mind is if someone hits you in the head with a two-by-four. The point is not to have a blank mind, but for your mind to become a clear still pool. To change the metphor slightly, Thomas Keating once explained it like this: The mind, our consciousness, is like a great river flowing along. If you are sitting on the bank of the river you will see all sorts of things float by: a tree limb, a riverboat, an empty soft drink can, a laughing group of people river tubing. You don't go out into the water and try to wrestle them ashore. You just watch them float by in the current. In the same way you cannot prevent thoughts from coming down the current of your consciousness, but you don't have to wade out into the river and grapple with them. You can just let them float by. The point is not to stop thoughts, but rather to not engage or pursue them.

COUNTING BREATH

One way of calming and stilling the mind is to count the breath, count one on inhalation and two on exhalation, or count each breath up to ten by starting with one on the first inhalation and two on the exhalation. After a few days count only on the inhalation. Eventually you stop counting, simply follow, and are gently conscious of your breathing. This has the effect of calming emotions and stilling all the reasoning and thinking that takes place at the more superficial levels, and helps you to let go of thoughts rather than engaging and becoming entangled with them. I mention the breath as a way of quieting the mind because that is the way I first learned. However, there are other ways of facilitating quiet prayer and you will have to choose the one that works best for you.

YOUR CENTERING WORD

Basil Pennington suggested that we choose what will be to us a sacred word. It is important that this word really represents our intention to be with God, and our consent to God's presence and action within us. The sacred word should, therefore, be chosen during a time of brief prayer in which we ask the Holy Spirit to guide us in choosing the word most suitable for us. Examples of the words we might choose are: "Lord," "Jesus," "Abba," "Amma," "grace," "peace," "mercy," or "amen." Rather than a single word, it could be a short phrase like: "I wait for the Lord," "I am with you always," "I seek Thy face," or "Come Lord Jesus." It is fine to change your word, but it should not be changed during contemplation since that engages active thought.

So, rather than following your breath, silently introduce your chosen word which symbolizes your consent to God's presence and your desire to be with God. Repeating your word, like counting your breath, will help to calm anxieties and decrease thinking until even your word or phrase drops away and you sit in complete inner silence. Whenever you begin to engage with a thought rather than simply letting it float by, return to repeating your sacred word or following your breath as a way of letting go or disengaging. Do not, however, get caught up in banishing thoughts as the goal of centering prayer. Much of the time it will be, as William Johnston notes, "At one level, a deep level, you are enjoying the sense of loving presence, while at a more superficial level thoughts are coming and going."[5] Pay no attention to the coming or going of thoughts. All that matters is your intention to be present with God. Continue to use the sacred word to reassert that intention. If there are ten thousand times you are distracted and you return to your original intention each time, this is a great success, for isn't that the essence of the spiritual life—constantly returning to our original intention to love God and the Christ whom God sent and revealed in the beauty of the Holy Spirit? As you practice this prayer of quiet, you may enter a deep unitive silence where you know the eter-

---

5. Johnston, *Being in Love*, 60–61.

It's Easier Than You Think

nal love of God for which there are no words. We can conclude with Thomas Keating that such prayer is in harmony with all the spiritual disciplines in that all "... are based on the hypothesis that there is something we can do to enter upon the journey to divine union once we have been touched by the realization that such a state exists.[6]

ENDING

At the end of a time of contemplative prayer, remain sitting quietly with eyes closed for a moment or two. You can end with a simple prayer of gratitude, or begin to pray with words either silently or out loud.

The minimum time recommended for contemplative prayer is twenty to thirty minutes once a day to begin with; you can add a second sitting later. It is suggested you purchase or download some sort of timer so that you are not distracted by watching the time. Some people will attempt to enter the silence for a few minutes, and then quit because, as they put it, "Nothing has happened." Contemplative prayer takes time. Frequently, I find the last two or three minutes the most valuable. But it takes all the other minutes to come to that place. Each sitting should allow enough time for the silence to grow and deepen. You could begin, then, by lighting your candle, centering down, meditating in the sense of reading and praying Scripture, practicing contemplation, and end with silently saying your prayers or colloquy. That entire exercise might take from forty-five minutes to an hour. Following is a simple step-by-step description of contemplative prayers for those who are trying to get started. This penultimate footnote contains a short list of books, all by recognized Christian authors, for beginners, though as for that we are all novices.[7]

---

6. Keating, *Open Mind, Open Heart*, 34.

7. Foster, *Celebration of Discipline*; Pennington, *Centering Prayer*; Willard, *Spirit of the Disciplines*. Anonymous, *Cloud of Unknowing* and *the Book of Privy Counselling*. Merton, *What is Contemplation?*; Main, *Way of Unknowing*.

CHECKLIST FOR CONTEMPLATIVE PRAYER

The following is a simple review and checklist for practicing contemplative prayer:

1) Sitting: (a) You may sit in a full Lotus or half Lotus position, on a mat with legs crossed, on a prayer cushion, on a prayer bench or on a chair. (b) How you sit doesn't much matter except that you should make sure your back is straight and if you are sitting in a chair that your feet are flat on the floor. (c) Hands may rest lightly in your lap, or on your thighs with palms turned up as a sign of receptiveness or with the right hand resting on the left, thumb-tips lightly touching.

2) Light a candle: (a) Say a short prayer as you do so, welcoming God's presence, asking that God will fill your heart as you now create space in it, or (b) dedicate this time to Christ; for example, "O Lord may my prayers rise up to you as the light of this candle forever reaches up to you."

3) Centering down, especially in the beginning: (a) Do a progressive muscle relaxation exercise in which you scan your entire body for any tension and let it go. (b) Inhale deeply, hold your breath to the count of five, and then sigh it all out. (c) Listen to a piece of music that is calming and peaceful, such as "Für Elise," "Elvira," John Michael Talbot's "The Quiet Side," or maybe Gregorian chants. (d) Pray with your imagination so that you feel yourself sinking deeper and deeper into the safe and peaceful presence of God.

4) Read Scripture: (a) A short meaningful verse for you or a Psalm (a traditional one from the Old Testament or see *Psalms for Praying* by Nan Merrill) or do ten minutes of *lectio divina*.

5) Introduce your sacred word and sit for twenty minutes: (a) When you become aware of pursuing or entertaining a thought, begin to repeat your word. (b) John Main suggested repeating your word continuously throughout the twenty-minute sit, but do what works best for you. (c) Main

It's Easier Than You Think

also strongly suggested using the word *"maranatha"*, an Aramaic word (1 Cor 16:22) meaning, "Come, Lord," because he thought its rhythm and sound helpful to meditation.

6) At the end of twenty minutes (you should be able to find a helpful bell or gong app) slowly and quietly open your eyes: (a) Read or repeat a Scripture verse; (b) say a prayer of gratitude; or (c) otherwise pray discursively before putting out your candle and going about the other business of the day.

THE PRAYER OF OCEANIC AWARENESS

I end with a personal note. I was doing a year-long chaplain residency in a large urban hospital. One of our responsibilities was to be in the emergency room when someone who had "cored" (who had a heart attack or wasn't breathing) was brought in, and then to be with the family as it arrived and gathered in a private waiting room. There might be several such incidents, and deaths, in a single day or night. After only about the third day I realized as I stood there watching the emergency room doctor and the nurses do everything they could to resuscitate someone whose heart had stopped that I was so tense that even my toes were curled inside my shoes. It came to me in that moment that I probably could not physically survive a year of that kind of stress and that it wouldn't be long before I was the one on the table. With that realization came another moment of spiritual clarity. I saw that the best thing I could do for any patient, the doctors, or the families I would work with, was to be as much of a peaceful, non-anxious, centered presence as I possibly could, to practice contemplative prayer, holding everyone and everything, silently and wordlessly in the love of God which, like the air we breathe, is all around and in us for the Spirit is the breath of the mystic (Gen 2:7; John 20:22). In the *Cadfael Chronicles* there is this wonderful description of the Benedictine monk, Brother Cadfael, praying for those caught up in the darkness, confusion, grief, and pain of a tragic death:

> He prayed as he breathed forming no words and making no specific requests, only holding in his heart, like broken birds in cupped hands, all these people who were in distress or in grief...[8]

Contemplative prayer, then, can become this wordless, silent, and constant holding of all things in love, while simultaneously knowing we are held in the cupped hands of divine love, presence, and sacred mystery.

For half of my life I have now lived within five to ten minutes of the Pacific Ocean or one of its bays. I love the ocean. Even on those days when I don't actually catch a glimpse of it and it doesn't enter my conscious thoughts, I am still aware, on another level, that it is there in power and beauty. Christian spirituality is like that. It's about always being aware, regardless of what is going on at the more superficial levels of our being, of the mysterious reality and presence of God. The practice of Christian contemplation or meditation, really of any prayer, is the practice of the presence of God so that eventually, whether we are explicitly thinking of God at any given moment, there is a constant awareness of the light, love, and life of Christ within us.

---

8. Peters, *Morbid Taste for Bones*, 122.

EPILOGUE

Those who doom themselves to this trial, this terrible school of life, do so voluntarily in the hope that after the long trial they will achieve self-conquest, self-mastery, to such a degree that they will finally, through a whole life's obedience attain to perfect freedom—that is freedom from themselves—and avoid the lot of those who live their lives without finding themselves in themselves.

From *The Brothers Karamazov*

Then Jesus told his disciples, "If any want to become my followers, let them deny themselves and take up their cross and follow me. For those who want to save their life will lose it, and those who lose their life for my sake will find it. For what will it profit them if they gain the whole world but forfeit their life? Or what will they give in return for their life?

From *The Gospel the According to Matthew* 16:24–26

Bibliography

Anonymous. *The Cloud of Unknowing* and *The Book of Privy Counselling*. Edited by William Johnston. Garden City NY: Doubleday, 1973.

———. "The Nine Ways of Prayer of St. Dominic." http://www.nashvilledominican.org/our-vowed-life/st-dominic/nine-ways-of-prayer.

Armstrong, Karen. *Visions of God: Four Medieval Mystics and Their Writings.* New York: Bantam, 1994.

Armstrong, Regis J., et al., eds. *Francis of Assisi—The Saint: Early Documents.* New York: Franciscan Institute of St. Bonaventure University, 1999.

Augustine. *Augustine's Confessions.* Grand Rapids, MI: Sovereign Grace, 1971.

Barry, William, SJ. *God and You: Prayer as Personal Relationship.* New York: Paulist, 1987.

———. *Paying Attention to God: Discernment in Prayer.* Notre Dame: Ave Maria, 1992.

Blake, William. "Auguries of Innocence." In *The Pocket Book of Verse: Great English and American Poems*, edited by M. E. Speare, 86. New York: Washington Square, 1943.

Browning, Elizabeth Barrett. *Aurora Leigh.* New York: C. S. Francis, 1857.

Buber, Martin. *"I and Thou:" A New Translation With a Prologue "I and You" and Notes.* Translated by Walter Kaufmann. New York: Charles Scribner's Sons, 1970.

Clinebell, Howard. J. *Basic Types of Pastoral Counseling: New Resources for Ministering to the Troubled.* Nashville: Abingdon, 1966.

Cobb, John, Jr. *Jesus' Abba: The God Who has Not Failed.* Minneapolis: Fortress, 2015.

Delahoyde, Michael. "The Medieval Period: Introduction." https://public.wsu.edu/~delahoyd/medieval/medieval_intro.html.

Downing, David C. *Into the Region of Awe: Mysticism in C. S. Lewis.* Downers Grove, IL: InterVarsity, 2005.

Eaton, John. *The Contemplative Face of Old Testament Wisdom: In the Context of World Religions.* London: SCM, 1989.

Egan, Harvey D. *Karl Rahner: Mystic of Everyday Life.* New York: Crossroad, 1998.

Bibliography

———. *What are They Saying about Mysticism?* New York: Paulist, 1982.
Eliot, T. S. *Four Quartets: The Centenary Edition*. San Diego: Harcourt, Brace Jovanovich, 1971.
Fenelon, Francois. *Let Go: To Get Real Peace and Joy*. Pittsburgh: Banner, 1973.
Foster, Richard. *The Celebration of Discipline: The Path to Spiritual Growth*. San Francisco: Harper and Row, 1978.
Gregory I. *The Book of Pastoral Rule and Selected Epistles of Pope St. Gregory I (The Great)*. Translated by James Barmby and edited by Paul A. Boer, Sr. Dublin: Veritati Splendor, 2012.
Gunther, Margaret. *The Practice of Prayer: The New Church Teaching Series, Vol. 4*. Cambridge, MA: Cowley, 1980.
Hamer, Dean. *The God Gene: How Faith is Hardwired into Our Genes*. New York: Doubleday, 2004.
Hart, Larry. *The Annunciation*. Eugene, OR: Wipf and Stock, 2017.
Hart, Lawrence D. *Alleluia is the Song of the Desert: An Exercise for Lent and Other Sacred Times*. Cambridge, MA: Cowley, 2004.
———. *A Little Book of Sanity: Finding Serenity in the Age of Anxiety*. Encinitas, CA: The Omega Project, 2010.
Hernandez, Will. *Mere Spirituality: The Spiritual Life According to Henri Nouwen*. London: SPCK, 2016.
Heschel, Abraham Joshua. *Quest for God: Studies in Prayer and Symbolism*. New York: Crossroad, 1993.
Imof, Paul, and Hubert Biallowons, eds. *Karl Rahner in Dialogue*. New York: Crossroad, 1986.
Johnson, Todd E. "Life as Prayer: The Development of Evelyn Underhill's Spirituality." https://fullerstudio.fuller.edu/life-as-prayer-the-development-of-evelyn-underhills-spirituality.
Johnston, William. *Being in Love: The Practice of Christian Prayer*. London: Harper-Collins Religious, 1988.
———. *Lord Teach Us to Pray: Christian Zen and the Inner Eye of Love*. London: Harper-Collins, 1990.
———. *The Mysticism of the Cloud of Unknowing*. Reprint. Trabuco Canyon, CA: Source, 1992.
———. *Silent Music: The Source of Meditation*. New York: Harper and Row, 1979.
Jonas, Robert A. "Christian Prayer: Silence and Dancing Between Knowing and Unknowing," http://www.emptybell.org/methods.html.
Jones, Cheslyn, et al., eds. *The Study of Spirituality*. New York: Oxford University Press, 1986.
Jones, E. Stanley. *The Way*. Nashville: Abingdon, 1946.
Julian of Norwich. *Revelations of Divine Love*. Edited by Grace Warrack. Overland Park, KS: Digireads/ Neeland Media, 2013.
Kaplan, Aryeh. *The Bible and Meditation*. York Beach, ME: Samuel Weisner, 1978.

Bibliography

Keating, Thomas. *The Contemplative Dimension of the Gospel*. New York: Continuum, 1994.

———. *Open Mind, Open Heart: The Contemplative Dimension of the Gospel*. New York: Continuum, 1994.

Knight, George A. F. *The Daily Bible Study Series: Psalms, Volume 1*. Philadelphia: Westminster, 1982.

Laird, Martin, OSA. *Into the Silent Land: A Guide to the Christian Practice of Contemplation*. Oxford: Oxford University Press, 2006.

Lane, George A. *Christian Spirituality: An Historical Sketch*. Chicago: Loyola, 1984.

Lewis, C. S. *Surprised by Joy: The Shape of My Early Life*. New York: Harcourt Brace Jovanovich, 1955.

Main, John. *Monastery Without Walls*. London: Canterbury, 2006.

———. *The Way of Unknowing: Expanding Spiritual Horizons through Meditation*. Norwich, UK: Canterbury, 2011.

Maurice, Frederick Denison, ed. *The Life of Frederick Denison Maurice Chiefly Told in His Own Letters*: Vol. 1. New York: Charles Scribner's Son, 1884.

May, Gerald. *The Awakened Heart*. New York: Harper Collins, 1991.

———. *Will & Spirit: A Contemplative Psychology*. New York: Harper and Row, 1982.

McGinn, Bernard. *Essential Writings of Christian Mysticism*. New York: The Modern Library, 2006.

———. *The Flowering of Mysticism: Men and Women in the New Mysticism 1200–1350. The Presence of God, Vol. 3. A History of Western Christian Mysticism*. New York: Crossroad, 1998.

———. *The Foundations of Mysticism: The Presence of God, Vol. 1: A History of Western Christian Mysticism*. New York: Crossroad, 1994.

———. *The Growth of Christian Mysticism: The Presence of God, Vol. 2: A History of Western Christian Mysticism: Gregory the Great through the 12th Century*. New York: Crossroad, 1994.

Merton, Thomas. *Contemplative Prayer*. Garden City, NY: Doubleday, 1971.

———. *A Course in Christian Mysticism*. Edited by Jon M. Sweeney. Collegeville, MN: Liturgical, 2017.

———. *Love and Living*. Edited by Naomi Burton Stone and Patrick Hart. New York: Harcourt, 1979.

———. *What is Contemplation?* Springfield, IL: Templegate, 1978.

Merton, Thomas, ed. *The Wisdom of the Desert: Sayings From the Desert Fathers of the Fourth Century*. New York: James Laughlin, 1960.

Metz, Johannes B. *Poverty of Spirit*. New York: Paulist, 1968.

Mulholland, M. Robert. *Shaped By The Word: The Power of Scripture in Spiritual Transformation*. Nashville: The Upper Room, 1985.

Nouwen, Henri J. M. *Letters to Mark About Jesus*. New York: Harper and Row, 1985.

———. *Making All Things New: An Invitation to the Spiritual Life*. San Francisco: Harper and Collins, 1981.

Bibliography

———. *Out of Solitude: Three Meditations on the Christian Life*. Notre Dame: Ave Maria, 1974.

———. *The Selfless Way of Christ: Downward Mobility and the Spiritual Life*. Maryknoll, NY: Orbis, 2007.

Peck, M. Scott. *People of the Lie: The Hope For Healing Human Evil*. New York: Simon and Schuster, 1983.

Pennington, M. Basil. *Centering Prayer: Renewing an Ancient Christian Prayer Form*. New York: Doubleday Image, 1980.

Peters, Ellis. *A Morbid Taste for Bones and the Cadfael Chronicles*. New York: Warner, 1977.

Plantinga, Alvin. *Warranted Christian Belief*. New York: Oxford University Press, 2000.

Rahner, Karl. *On Prayer*. Collegeville, MN: Liturgical, 1968.

Ricoeur, Paul. *The Symbolism of Evil*. Translated by Emerson Buchanan. Boston: Beacon, 1967.

Robinson, Marilynne. *Gilead*. New York: Farrar, Straus, and Giroux, 2004.

Sangster, W. E. *The Secret of the Radiant Life: A Step-by-Step Guide and Twelve Spiritual Exercises*. Nashville: Abingdon, 1957.

Sapp, Stephen. *Sexuality, the Bible and Science*. Philadelphia: Fortress, 1977.

Schweitzer, Albert. *The Mysticism of Paul the Apostle*. Translated by William Montgomery. Baltimore: The John Hopkins University Press, 1998.

Solzhenitsyn, Aleksandr I. *The Gulag Archipelago*, Vol. 2. Translated by Thomas P. Whitney. New York: Harper and Row, 1974.

Steindl-Rast, David. *Gratefulness: The Heart of Prayer*. New York: Paulist, 1984.

Stewart, James S. *A Man in Christ*. Reprint. Grand Rapids, MI: Baker, 1975.

Suzuki, Shunryu. *Zen Mind, Beginner's Mind*. New York: Weatherhill, 1986.

Teasedale, Wayne. *Bede Griffiths: An Introduction to His Interspiritual Thought*. Woodstock, VT: SkyLight Paths, 2003.

Therese of Lisieux. *The Little Way for Every Day: Thoughts from Therese of Lisieux*. Translated by Francis Broome. New York: Paulist, 1989.

———. *Story of a Soul: The Autobiography of Saint Therese of Lisieux*. Translated by John Clarke. Washington, DC: ICS, 2017.

Thornton, Martin. *Christian Proficiency*. London: SPCK, 1961.

———. *My God: A Reappraisal of Normal Religious Experience*. London: Hodder and Stoughton, 1974.

Tillich, Paul. *The Shaking of the Foundations*. New York: Charles Scribner's Sons, 1948.

Ulanov, Barry. *Prayers of St. Augustine*. Minneapolis: Seabury, 1983.

Underhill, Evelyn. *Mysticism: A Study in the Nature and Development of Man's Spiritual Consciousness*. New York: New American Library, 1974.

———. *The Spiritual Life: Four Broadcast Talks*. London: Hodder & Stoughton, 1937.

Vest, Norvene. *Preferring Christ: A Devotional Commentary on the Rule of St. Benedict*. Harrisburg, PA: Morehouse, 1990.

Willard, Dallas. *The Spirit of the Disciplines: Understanding How God Changes Lives.* New York: Harper and Row, 1988.
Woods, Richard. *Christian Spirituality: God's Presence through the Ages.* Allen, TX: Christian Classics, 1989.
Wright, N. T. *Jesus and the Victory of God: Christian Origins and the Question of God, Vol. 2.* Minneapolis: Fortress, 1996.
Yeats, William Butler. "Vacillation." In *Selected Poems and Two Plays of William Butler Yeats,* edited by M. L. Rosenthal, 135. New York: Macmillian, 1962.
Zorilla, Hugo. *Saint John of the Cross from Anabaptist Spirituality.* Fresno, CA: self-published, 1993.

www.ingramcontent.com/pod-product-compliance
Lightning Source LLC
Chambersburg PA
CBHW050837160426
43192CB00011B/2058